Copyright Page

This book reflects the author's personal journey, beliefs, and understanding at the time of writing. It is offered in humility and faith, not as doctrine, but as an invitation to reflect, surrender, and develop a relationship with God.

ISBN: 978-1-7374732-3-7

Library of Congress Control Number: Not assigned

First Edition

Printed in the United States of America

Lay Down Your Burdens

Finding Peace, Healing, and Trust in God Through Surrender

Kyle Charles Becker

"My grace is sufficient for thee." — 2 Corinthians 12:9

Table of Contents

Introduction

Man is that he might have joy.

This truth stands at the center of God's plan for His children, even when life is heavy and suffering feels unavoidable—even when life is dark and the night seems as though it will last forever. Much of our pain persists not because joy is withheld, but because we carry things that block us from receiving it. There are things within us that separate us from the sunlight of His Spirit. There are things within us that separate us from God.

These things within us sustain much of our suffering. They deepen our pain and give rise to fear, doubt, anxiety, and worry. They feed shame, guilt, regret, and despair. Often, the darkness we experience in life is not caused by God's absence, but by our failure to recognize what we are carrying—or our unwillingness, or inability, to let go of what has weighed us down for so long.

Are you lost?
Are you afraid?
Are you in pain?
Are you suffering?

Do you feel there must be more to life than what you have been living? Has the weight of all your days pressed heavily upon your soul? Have the decisions and experiences of your life left you longing for peace, rest, and serenity?

Matthew 11:28–30 (KJV)

Jesus said:

"Come unto me, all ye that labour and are heavy laden, and I will give you rest.

Take my yoke upon you, and learn of me; for I am meek and lowly in heart: and ye shall find rest unto your souls.

For my yoke is easy, and my burden is light."

This book is a guide to laying down your burdens and finding rest unto your soul. Within these pages, you will begin to identify the things you have carried—often unknowingly—that have weighed upon your spirit for much of your life. You will learn tools, disciplines, and practices that help you lay those burdens down and allow God to remove them in His way, in His time.

This book is meant to draw you closer to God, Jesus Christ, and the Holy Spirit by helping you remove the inner resistance, fear, and barriers that have kept you from fully receiving Their presence. It is an invitation to open your eyes that you might see, open your ears that you might hear, and soften your heart so that God may breathe into you His healing and transformative love.

You will learn the mental, emotional, and spiritual understanding and postures necessary—not as ways to coerce God, but to deepen communion with Him and align your will with His will, His plan, and His timing.

This book will walk you through a loving moral inventory—not to condemn you but to illuminate the things within you that are no longer serving you. You will gently examine your past to uncover the roots of pain and suffering, bringing into awareness those things that separate you from the sunlight of His Spirit. You will be guided through a process of repentance, forgiveness, and release—learning not only how to forgive others, but how to forgive yourself.

You will learn to love God and humanity as He loves you and all His children. And you will learn to see life as He does—through the eyes of eternity.

I humbly and meekly invite you to take this walk with me. You deserve to feel joy, peace, love, and security in your life. God desires these things for you—and much more. Together, with the help of a loving God, our Savior and Redeemer Jesus Christ, and the guiding influence of the Holy Spirit, there is nothing beyond our reach.

Part One:
The Burdens We Carry

We begin this blessed journey by bringing awareness—and light—to the things that have separated us from the sunlight of His Spirit. Together, we will uncover the burdens we carry, the weights that dim our connection with God and cloud the radiance of His presence in our lives.

This exploration will unfold across three chapters: Emotional Burdens, Mental Burdens, and Spiritual Burdens. Each chapter is designed to deepen our understanding of what may be standing between us and God.

This will not be an exhaustive list of all possible burdens, but it will focus on some very powerful ones. The purpose of Part One is to bring awareness to—and help you recognize—the burdens we will be working to lay down throughout this book. We will explore these in much greater depth later, when we complete a Loving Moral Inventory.

You may not recognize yourself in every burden described, and that is perfectly natural. This is not a checklist of shortcomings, but a mirror. It offers guidance as we search our hearts, minds, and spirits, identifying what no longer serves our growth or our closeness to God.

Through this process, we begin the sacred work of offering ourselves to our Creator—that He might do with us, and build within us, what He will—removing those things within us that are unpleasing to Him and that separate us from His love, peace, and joy.

There is a lot to this chapter. Feel free to pause and take a break. If you can, allow each section the breath and space it needs to unfold within you. There is no right or wrong way to go about this, just know that this isn't a race; God's patience is infinite and He loves you so very much.

Chapter 1 - Emotional Burdens

Core Burden: Fear

For most of my life, I have lived with—and been influenced by—fear.

Some of that fear showed up quietly, like being shy and afraid to ask out the girl I had a crush on. I was fifteen. She was so beautiful. We had great chemistry, but before I got up the courage to ask her out, my best friend did. And that was it. That became a regret that affected me for decades to come.

Other fears were far more consuming, like the fear of speaking in front of an audience. I worked in sales, and this fear kept me from progressing in my career.

I feared that I was not good enough, affecting everything from getting the girl, to getting the promotion, to not starting my own business.

I feared that one day I would be cast aside and abandoned, causing me to be clingy and controlling in my relationships.

I feared that if you truly knew who I was—or if I failed to be who I thought you wanted me to be—you would reject me, causing me to be dishonest with others, to lie so that I might fit in, never truly being comfortable as I truly was.

(Matthew 6:25)

"Therefore, I say unto you, take no thought for your life, what ye shall eat, or what ye shall drink; nor yet for your body, what ye shall put on."

I feared that I was trapped in my current career and incapable of becoming anything more. I feared that my employer would eventually realize they did not need me—that I was not as capable or valuable as they believed—which kept me anxious and ever vigilant in everything that I did. It was exhausting.

I feared that the life I had worked so hard to build could be taken away from me at any moment. I felt as though I had no other prospects, my life always existing in some precarious position, one misstep away from collapse. I overcompensated for this in every possible way—lying, cheating, and deceiving—all so that I might hold on to that which, in my mind, was always slipping away.

"Behold the fowls of the air: for they sow not, neither do they reap, nor gather into barns; yet your heavenly Father feedeth them. Are ye not much better than they?" (Matthew 6:26)

I feared being alone—afraid that I would not be okay if that day ever came, believing that if I became alone, I would always be alone; that the relationship I was in, even though imperfect and filled with pain, could be the best I was going to get, so I might as well grin and bear it.

I feared failing as a father and letting my sons down. I feared that I would somehow fail them entirely. I was young, unprepared, and deeply aware of my own shortcomings. I believed that I simply was not good enough. This made me an overbearing and controlling father, never truly allowing them to fully be who they wanted to be, always measuring them against an impossible standard I thought I needed to hold them to in order to be a good father.

(Matthew 6:27)

"Which of you by taking thought can add one cubit unto his stature?"

At its core, my fear revolved around two things: losing something I believed I needed in order to feel safe and happy or never receiving something I believed I needed to feel whole and secure. I lived in a constant state of anxiety—always worried, always anticipating loss, always trying to control outcomes and variables beyond my reach.

At that time, I knew little of God's will and even less of faith or hope. I constantly struggled, clawed, scratched, and sought to control all the details—every person, place, and situation in my life. This put me in constant conflict with others and in constant conflict with myself.

This is not to say that my life lacked goodness. I have lived a life full of blessings and meaningful moments. But beneath it all, there was a persistent undercurrent of insecurity—one that kept me striving to stay in control, yet never truly at peace. Fear kept me vigilant, guarded, and exhausted.

(Matthew 6:28–29)

"And why take ye thought for raiment? Consider the lilies of the field, how they grow; they toil not, neither do they spin. Even Solomon in all his glory was not arrayed like one of these."

To one degree or another, fear diminished the quality of every area of my life. My fear of not being enough wounded those I loved the most, as I sought validation from them—hoping they might give me what only God could provide.

I looked outward for reassurance that I was okay, that I mattered, that I was secure. It was an impossible weight to put on the shoulders of anyone. My incessant demands, meant to make me feel whole and worthy, drove the ones I loved into the ground. I hurt the ones that I love because I did not think I was enough.

Fear, a state opposing love and devoid of faith, has played a larger role in creating many other character defects and personality flaws. Things like arrogance, self-righteousness, judgmentalism, defensiveness, dishonesty, perfectionism, impatience, intolerance, anger, pessimism, neediness, and many others are responses I developed because of fear.

(Matthew 6:30)

"Wherefore, if God so clothe the grass of the field, which today is, and tomorrow is cast into the oven, shall He not much more clothe you, O ye of little faith?"

Through diligence and hard work, fasting and prayer, and through faith in His love for me, I began to recognize my fears for what they were. I learned to see how they shaped my thoughts, influenced my behaviors, and quietly governed my decisions. As I brought those fears into the light, their power over me began to weaken.

Slowly, those fears loosened their hold on me. In their place came peace, serenity, hope, confidence, and faith. Becoming aware of my fears—and how they were manifesting in my life—brought me closer to God than I had ever been before.

(Matthew 6:31–34)

"Therefore take no thought, saying, What shall we eat? or, What shall we drink? or, Wherewithal shall we be clothed?"

"For your heavenly Father knoweth that ye have need of all these things."

"But seek ye first the kingdom of God, and his righteousness; and all these things shall be added unto you."

"Take therefore no thought for the morrow: for the morrow shall take thought for the things of itself."

Fear is not a warning but a heavy burden, keeping us anchored to control rather than trust in God. Fear is no longer needed. Life is not sustained by vigilance or self-protection, but by God. When fear is surrendered—not resisted, not managed, but released—the soul is freed to move forward in trust, and life can finally be received as it was meant to be.

Core Burden: Grief and Loss

Sorrow and grief are woven into the human experience. They are inevitable. There is no bypassing them and no rushing through them. Scripture does not minimize loss, nor does it pretend that pain should disappear quickly. Instead, it allows space for mourning and acknowledges the depth of the human heart.

We must allow ourselves to feel the feelings we need to feel and permit them to run their course. Grief is not a failure of faith. What we must remember—especially in our darkest moments—is that the Lord loves us and is always ready to step into our lives and share this burden with us.

(Lamentations 3:31–32)

"For the Lord will not cast off for ever: But though He cause grief, yet will He have compassion according to the multitude of his mercies."

We often hear the saying that God will not give us anything we cannot handle. I would gently suggest that He does give us things we cannot handle—so that we will turn to Him for His help, His love, and His grace. He desires to be there for us as any loving parent would.

Grief itself is not sin, or weakness, and does not separate us from Him, but the loss of a loved one is often one of those burdens we simply cannot carry on our own. And that is okay, because we were never meant to. We are never alone. He is always with us. We can absolutely choose to lay that burden down and allow God's perfect love to comfort and heal us.

As I look back over the moments of my life, I see a common thread woven through them all: the Hand of God and the steady presence of a loving Brother and Savior, Jesus Christ. I see the difficult seasons that overwhelmed me—times that were far too much for me to handle—and I see how God answered my prayers in those moments. Always. He never forsook me, the proof of which is that I am still here writing this book. I'm still breathing. My heart still beats in my chest. He was always there to protect me, to strengthen me, and to hold me up when I could not stand on my own.

(2 Corinthians 1:3)

“Blessed be God, even the Father of our Lord Jesus Christ, the Father of mercies, and the God of all comfort.”

I remember my grandmother Hazel telling me—then a seventeen-year-old boy in the midst of the darkest time of his life—“Your Heavenly Father loves you, Kyle. Everything is going to be okay.” Those words carried light into a season of deep darkness, and they have remained with me ever since.

In our darkest hours, we must draw near to God. We must seek His comfort and His love. We must hold to faith—faith that this too shall pass, that the pain is not permanent, and that healing is possible, even when the suffering feels unbearable.

(Matthew 5:4)

“Blessed are they that mourn: for they shall be comforted.”

Prayer can help. I know this because I have been there—praying through the night, pleading that He would remove the pain, that He would heal my heart, and that His comfort, peace, and grace would rest upon me. These were prayers offered through mighty tears and an aching desire to simply not hurt anymore.

Scripture speaks tenderly to such prayers:

(Psalm 34:17–18)

“The righteous cry, and the Lord heareth, and delivereth them out of all their troubles.
The Lord is nigh unto them that are of a broken heart; and saveth such as be of a contrite spirit.”

And in those prayers—though the pain did not always leave immediately—I was never left alone. God was there. He always is. And when things seemed as though they could not get any worse, that is often when His peace would come. When the night was at its darkest, the dawn was already drawing near.

If you are dealing with grief and loss, please know that this too shall pass. All things do under heaven. I don't say that to diminish what you are going through, I say that to let you know that His comfort is there if you want it.

Death is not the end, but the beginning. In eternity, all things are made whole, all wounds are healed, and all that is broken is restored.

Ecclesiastes 3:1–4 (KJV)

To every thing there is a season,
and a time to every purpose under the heaven:

A time to be born, and a time to die;
a time to plant, and a time to pluck up that which is planted;

A time to kill, and a time to heal;
a time to break down, and a time to build up;

A time to weep, and a time to laugh;
a time to mourn, and a time to dance.

Core Burdens: Anger and Resentment

We will touch briefly on anger before turning our attention to resentment, which can be understood as internalized, unresolved anger directed toward external people, places, events, or institutions. Self-directed unresolved anger—often experienced as regret or shame—will be addressed in the next section.

Let us be honest: we are going to get angry. Regardless of our level of emotional, mental, or spiritual development, life will present moments that provoke us. Anger itself is inevitable. What matters is how we respond to it—how we choose to act upon it, both outwardly and inwardly.

(Ephesians 4:26)

"Be ye angry, and sin not."

There are many reasons anger may arise in our lives:

Emotional pain caused by words, actions, or neglect

Betrayal by someone trusted

Feeling dismissed, misunderstood, or invalidated

Being treated unfairly or unjustly

Seeing wrongdoing go unaddressed

Expectations of people, life, or God that were not fulfilled

Believing things should have gone differently

Being ignored, belittled, or taken for granted

Feeling unseen or unappreciated

Childhood hurts

Old losses or betrayals

Trauma that was never named or healed

Other people's driving

The list could go on and on.

It is not a bad thing to feel anger. Anger can be expressed in healthy ways, provided it does not lead us to harm ourselves or others or lead us to sin. Problems arise when anger is suppressed, rehearsed, or allowed to linger.

(James 1:20)

"For the wrath of man worketh not the righteousness of God."

When anger is not resolved, it often transforms into resentment. Resentment is anger that has been carried too long, something that we are choosing to hold onto. It settles into the heart and quietly influences our thoughts, behaviors, and relationships. Over time, it diminishes our peace, joy, love, and spiritual clarity.

Someone once said that holding a resentment is like drinking poison and expecting someone else to get sick. A resentment stains the soul, and until we make peace with it, it will continue to act upon us to our own detriment.

The key to resolving resentment is forgiveness.

(Ephesians 4:31–32)

"Let all bitterness, and wrath, and anger, and clamour, and evil speaking, be put away from you with all malice: And be ye kind one to another, tenderhearted, forgiving one another, even as God for Christ's sake hath forgiven you."

Later in this book, I will share practical strategies that can help you uncover and release the resentments you carry. It is possible to forgive everyone of every trespass—real or perceived. God will help you do it.

I have harbored many resentments in my own life.

There was a resentment I carried from third grade, after being beaten up on the playground. I held onto it for decades. It became the root of my fear of confrontation and quietly affected my life well into adulthood. A resentment held for more than thirty years still had the power to disturb my peace. I needed to forgive him.

There was the resentment I carried toward a babysitter who molested me. I was an innocent victim and had done nothing wrong. Yet I still needed to forgive—not to excuse the harm, but to free myself from the burden it placed on my emotional security and ability to love.

There was resentment toward a former friend who introduced me to hard drugs and a life of crime. He betrayed me, stole from me, and led me into darkness and shame. I needed to forgive him.

There was resentment toward the church I belonged to as a child. While no clear wrongdoing had occurred, the way I believed the church's rules were applied in my family left a lasting impression on me. As children, we can absorb resentments whether they are warranted or not. I needed to forgive the church, my parents, and the entire situation, because I had been wrong.

Later in this book, we will complete a Loving Moral Inventory, which will help uncover resentments—both obvious and hidden. Some are easy to identify. Others require effort, honesty, and the help of God, Jesus Christ, and the Holy Spirit.

It is my hope that this section has given you insight into anger and resentment. As we continue through this book, we will work diligently to help you find the willingness to forgive everyone in your life for all things, real or perceived.

Resentments are burdens that must be laid down. It is only by forgiving others that I have been forgiven. All the moments of my life have been forgiven by God and so can yours. And just as important, all the moments of my life have been forgiven by me. I have forgiven myself for all of it. A great blessing indeed.

(Matthew 6:14)

"For if ye forgive men their trespasses, your heavenly Father will also forgive you."

Core Burden: Regret

Regret is the pain of a road not taken—or one taken and wished undone. It is sorrow for words left unsaid, for love not expressed, for opportunities missed out of fear or confusion. It is the ache of a question that can no longer be answered, a moment that cannot be revisited, a past that cannot be relived.

Regret lives in time—a time that can feel cruel, endlessly reminding us of what might have been. Left unchecked, regret can become soul-crushing and life-altering.

Just as resentment is unresolved anger toward others, regret is unresolved anger turned inward—a self-directed resentment born of self-contempt or self-loathing. We punish ourselves for not knowing then what we know now, for falling short of who we believed we should have been.

The cure for regret is the same as the cure for resentment: forgiveness. In this case, self-forgiveness.

Later in this book, we will walk through practical ways to forgive ourselves after completing the Loving Moral Inventory.

I write this with tears of joy, because I have carried so many regrets. What I can tell you with certainty is that there is a solution. Every regret I have carried has been forgiven—by me—with the help of God. Through honesty, willingness, prayer, fasting, and grace, forgiveness is not only possible; it is life changing. You can lay these burdens down.

God sees us through the lens of eternity. To Him, we are already perfected and whole. It is we—bound by time—who continue to carry these burdens, often because we do not know how to lay them down, or because we believe we are somehow unworthy of forgiveness.

This truth bears repeating: you are a child of God. Your Heavenly Father loves you and desires that you might have joy.

Some of the things you regret may not have been mistakes at all. They may have been part of His plan—His hand guiding you, even when you could not see it. And even when we do stray, He continues to work in us and through us, guiding us—sometimes along a different path—to the same ultimate destination. God is like the North Star. No matter how far the wind pushes us off course, if we keep our eyes on Him, we can always adjust our sails and find our way home.

I have always been my own harshest critic. For much of my life, I believed I needed to be perfect to be accepted—to avoid rejection, to avoid failure. When I inevitably fell short, I crucified myself for it.

What I have learned through much prayer, hard spiritual work, pain, suffering, and sorrow is this: I am exactly as I am meant to be and exactly where I am meant to be, in this moment. If I could have been different, I would have been. I am perfectly imperfect—and lovable not in spite of my shortcomings, but often because of them.

I invite you to begin developing the willingness to forgive yourself, just as God already has. Through the Atonement of Christ all things have been forgiven. You did the best you could with what you had at the time.

Philippians 3:13–14

"Forgetting those things which are behind, and reaching forth unto those things which are before, I press toward the mark for the prize of the high calling of God in Jesus Christ"

Core Burden: Hopelessness

There came a point in my life when survival required me to be willing to change everything. I was losing a battle with alcoholism. There were whispers that I had a drinking problem, and everyone seemed to know—my boss, my closest friend, my brothers, my parents, my wife, my sons. My pride wouldn't let me accept the truth until it was too late. I was an alcoholic.

Alcoholism is a disease that has destroyed millions of lives. It is progressive, relentless, and merciless, leaving its sufferers unable to stop drinking no matter how desperately they want to quit. Slowly and steadily, it takes the body and the mind, unraveling everything in its path.

The final nine months of my drinking left me broken and frustrated every single day. Each morning I woke up determined not to drink—just for that day. And every night I found myself at home with a bottle, stunned and defeated. I wanted to stop but I couldn't. No matter how hard I tried, no matter how valiant the struggle, I was powerless to do anything about it.

I chose the bottle over a seventeen-year marriage, shattering a family of four. I lost my health, gained fifty pounds, I had begun bruising all over my body, and I lied about why. I called in sick weekly with made-up illnesses as my employer's patience wore thin. I was on the verge of losing my job, my home, and whatever remained of my dignity—living a life I didn't want and powerless to change it.

The night of my last drink began like so many others. I woke up determined that this would be the day. If I could get one day sober, I told myself, then maybe I could get two. Driving home, focused only on not buying a bottle, I pulled into a grocery store parking lot. Sitting there, I pleaded with myself: "Just go home. Don't go in. If you don't buy it, you won't drink."

I went inside anyway.

At home, I poured the bottle out without taking a drink—and that's when the insanity took over. A terrifying certainty settled in: if I didn't drink, I would die. My body burned. My mind screamed. It felt as though my world would collapse if I didn't have that first drink. I drove to another store and bought a bottle.

A couple of hours later, after drinking the entire bottle, I sat across from my seventeen-year-old son, filled with fear and desperation, I told him the truth—that I couldn't stop drinking, and that if I didn't get help, I was afraid I would drink myself to death. The look on his face, and the shame in my heart, were unbearable.

I went to my bedroom and called everyone I could think of. I called my mom, my brothers, my dad, my other son, my grandmother. No one answered. Panic set in. I collapsed on the bathroom floor, curled into myself, shaking, exhausted, trembling, and afraid. I cried the kind of cry that burns in your soul, a mighty cry that makes no sound. My disease had taken everything I was. Every promise to quit that ended in another drink stripped away a piece of my soul.

Lying there, I could see the future clearly. I couldn't stop. It was getting worse. I had already lost more than I could bear, and the disease was preparing to take even more. I was a man I didn't want to be, living a life I didn't want to live, terrified I would die a horrible alcoholic death.

In that moment, all hope was gone. It was the dark night of my soul. There was nothing I could do... There was nothing I could do.

So, I cried out desperately—praying as though my life depended on it:

"Please, Lord. Please. Please. Please. God, help me."

When the night is darkest, when hope has vanished and the weight is more than we can carry, that is often where God stands nearest—waiting patiently for the soul to be ready to receive the blessing He has already prepared for us.

When I couldn't cry any longer, a sense of peace fell over my body, mind, and soul. What I initially thought was just being exhausted and numb to the pain, in hindsight was the Grace of God. It was serenity. It was peace. In that moment I found the strength and a willingness to do whatever it took for as long as it took to not live that life any longer, to not be that man any longer.

Ever so quietly, but clear as anything I had ever witnessed, a voice in my head said,

"Call your stepmother… Call your stepmother."

I had never experienced anything like it.

I called and she answered. It was very late where they lived, but she answered. She tried to console me, but I couldn't stop crying. She handed the phone to my father, and it's as if he had been waiting and preparing his whole life to have this conversation with me.

He calmly presented me with options, making me feel like maybe—just maybe—I can get through this.

There was a feeling of great calm, and then there it was.
There was hope… finally, there was hope.

The dark night of my soul was about to end.
The sun was coming.

That was October 27th, 2013.

I have not had a drink since. God had taken the need from me, root and branch. I had been saved.

Throughout the Bible, God repeatedly saves His people when all hope seems lost. Again and again, individuals and entire nations find themselves trapped by enemies, by famine, by sin, by weakness, or by despair—with no power to rescue themselves.

The Israelites stand pinned between Pharaoh's army and the Red Sea, certain of death, until God parts the waters and makes a way where none existed (Exodus 14:10–22).

Jonah cries out from the depths, believing himself doomed, and God hears him and he is saved (Jonah 2:1–7).

Paul and Silas sit bound in a prison cell at midnight, and sang praises unto God, and God shakes the foundations and opens every door (Acts 16:25–26).

A woman long afflicted and beyond medical help reaches for Christ in desperation and is healed. (Mark 5:25–34).

Elijah, exhausted and despairing, asks God to let him die, and God answers not with rebuke, but with rest, sustenance, and direction and guidance (1 Kings 19:4–8).

Examples go on and on.

In these moments, deliverance comes not through human strength, but through God's will and grace. The pattern is consistent: when people are brought low enough to recognize their need for God, being humbled by their own shortcomings and the trials of life, He answers.

Sometimes He removes the burden entirely, other times He strengthens His children to endure until salvation comes. The biblical stories stand united in the fact that no situation is beyond God's power to redeem, and no soul is ever truly beyond hope.

If you are walking through the dark night of your soul, hang on—do not give up, and do not quit before the miracle happens. The miracle will come, just as it has countless times throughout human history for countless souls who are just like you.

Our Heavenly Father loves us, and He will always be there for us when we humbly turn to Him. It is in our weakness that His strength is made perfect. Trust in Him. Seek Him. Come unto Him humbly and meekly with all your burdens and allow Him to lift them from you—always according to His will, His plan, and in His perfect time.

And I pray:

"God, I come to You today with a heavy heart. I carry with me a pain that I no longer want to carry. I just don't want it any longer.

I don't know what to do about it. I don't know where to begin. My best understanding and effort have failed me.

God, please help me, that I might know You better, that I might learn of Your ways, that I might find a way to lay down these burdens.

God, please direct me, that I might set aside everything I know to be true about You and Your will and purpose for me in this life, that I might gain a better understanding, that I might begin to see Your wisdom in all of it, that I might begin to see that You have a plan for me that is greater than I could have ever designed on my own."

Chapter 2 - Mental Burdens

Core Burden: False Identity

What we believe to be true does not merely influence how we think or act; over time, it becomes who we believe ourselves to be.

Let us take a moment to define what a belief is and how the word will be used in this section. A belief can be understood as a state or habit of mind in which trust or confidence is placed in someone or something; something accepted as true; or a conviction regarding a statement or reality, often based on evidence.

As a state of mind, belief shapes how we perceive and respond to a situation. For example, believing we are insecure in a relationship leads to different thoughts, emotions, and behaviors than believing we are secure.

As a habit, beliefs become automatic. They quietly activate in certain circumstances, influencing our thoughts and reactions without conscious effort. While beliefs may shift depending on context or situation, they function in the same underlying way. Because beliefs are rooted in what we accept as true, many of the beliefs we live by are subjective—formed not only by facts, but by what we have come to believe is true, whether that perceived truth is accurate or not.

These beliefs shape our experience of reality and guide how we respond to life. Through them, we define ourselves and our lives. Depending on the results they produce, we may view them as helpful or harmful—if we are aware of them at all.

When we are unaware of our beliefs, we can see their effects without understanding their source. We observe the fruit, but not the tree from which it came. Once beliefs are brought into the light, they can be examined honestly to determine whether they draw us closer to our Savior or distance us from the sunlight of His Spirit.

Beliefs also strongly influence how we perceive reality through confirmation bias. Confirmation bias is the tendency to seek out, notice, and interpret information in ways that support what we already believe, while disregarding or minimizing information that challenges those beliefs. In this way, confirmation bias reinforces our existing view of the world.

Through this process, we tend to hear what we have conditioned ourselves to hear, see what we have conditioned ourselves to see, and feel what we have conditioned ourselves to feel. This pattern makes objectivity and change difficult. At a deep level, we seek stability, predictability, comfort, and safety—even when evidence suggests that change is needed.

I Am the Natural Man

Having been an imperfect natural man my whole life, I have been burdened with imperfect beliefs:

I am not enough.
I am unlovable.
I am broken.
I am a burden.
I am unwanted.
I am weak.
I am a failure.
I am defective.
I am unsafe.

I am alone.
I am undeserving.
I am flawed beyond repair.
I am powerless.
I am not worthy of love.

Many moments of my life have been filtered through these beliefs, and I have responded accordingly. My life today is, to some extent, a mirror image of them. Beliefs are self-fulfilling prophecies, reinforced by confirmation bias. As you read this list, consider how many of these beliefs have been active in your own life. What have been the results? What fruit have those trees produced?

Matthew 7:16–20 (KJV)

"Ye shall know them by their fruits. Do men gather grapes of thorns, or figs of thistles?
Even so every good tree bringeth forth good fruit; but a corrupt tree bringeth forth evil fruit.
A good tree cannot bring forth evil fruit, neither can a corrupt tree bring forth good fruit.
Every tree that bringeth not forth good fruit is hewn down, and cast into the fire.
Wherefore by their fruits ye shall know them."

What I would like to suggest is that perhaps there is a better way. We are not just flesh and bone; we also have a spirit. I can choose to identify with the natural man and all the beliefs that come with it, or I can choose to identify with the spirit and a whole different set of beliefs. I can choose to reframe I am a natural man having a spiritual experience to I am a spirit having a natural man experience. I believe the latter to be true, while the former is a limiting belief born of ignorance. For most of my life, I knew not what I did.

Luke 23:34 (KJV)

"Then said Jesus, Father, forgive them; for they know not what they do."

I Am Spirit

I have been on a journey of spiritual exploration and growth ever since I was saved from my alcoholism on that fateful night, October 27th, 2013. My path has not been a straight one. It has been slow and steady—two steps forward and one step back—marked by detours, significant setbacks, and occasional giant leaps forward. Slowly but surely, putting one foot in front of the other, I have traveled a great distance. Along this path, I have changed my entire outlook on life, largely because I have changed my core beliefs and what I identify myself to be.

I have accepted that one day I will indeed die—that this mortal life will pass—and I have made peace with that reality. I have accepted the frail and impermanent nature of this vessel for my soul. I have accepted the imperfect creation that is the natural man. Through this acceptance, I have begun to identify less and less with the natural man and to shift my understanding toward that of the spirit.

As I've grown in spirit and grown closer to our Creator, Jesus Christ, and the Holy Spirit, I have been blessed to view life through a totally different set of beliefs. I have, it seems, put on a new set of glasses.

I am a spirit having a natural man experience.

I am a Child of God.

My Heavenly Father loves me.

My Heavenly Father created me that I might have Joy.

In eternity I am forgiven all things.

I am perfectly lovable.

I am whole, at one with all things.

I am exactly as I am supposed to be, exactly at this moment, exactly as He created me to be.

I could not have been any other way or I would have been—God doesn't make mistakes.

I am never alone.

I am an instrument of His peace, love, and grace.

These are the filters through which I now view reality. As confirmation bias seeks supportive evidence for these beliefs, they continue to grow stronger and stronger. My life is peaceful now. My days are filled with joy. When presented with an obstacle, I know I can always turn to Him for help, and He will make all things right in accordance with His will. I see this obstacle or adversity as an opportunity to learn more about Him, draw near to Him, and love Him better. I believe in His plan for me, although I don't know what it is. I believe in His timing, although I am impatient. I believe in Eternal life, although nothing in this world confirms it.

Romans 8:16–17 (KJV)

"The spirit itself beareth witness with our spirit, that we are the children of God:
And if children, then heirs; heirs of God, and joint-heirs with Christ;

if so be that we suffer with Him, that we may be also glorified together."

There is so much I do not know—so much that has not yet been revealed to me. I strive daily to remain humble and teachable, praying to the Godhead for guidance, inspiration, and help in recognizing my weaknesses and errors in thinking. I know it is only by the grace of God that I have the blessings that I have in my life, and I try to keep this truth at the forefront of my mind. His will. His power. His blessings. His glory. Remembering these keeps me on the path.

Take a look at what you believe to be true. Take a look at your life—use it as a mirror to reveal yourself to yourself. Are you a natural man or woman, or are you an Eternal spirit, a beautiful child of God? Do you believe that your Heavenly Father loves you? Begin your journey today. Walk toward Him. He has prepared a path for you.

Proverbs 3:5–6 (KJV)

"Trust in the LORD with all thine heart;
and lean not unto thine own understanding.
In all thy ways acknowledge Him,
and He shall direct thy paths."

Core Burden: Imperfect Beliefs of God

I feel it is supremely important and necessary for each of us to develop and nurture our own personal relationship with God, Jesus Christ, and the Holy Spirit—to not simply take someone else's word for it. We need to come unto Him and rely upon His perfect understanding, for no one knows what is best for us better than He does. He has seen our whole life in totality through the eyes of eternity. Put your trust and faith in Him, and He will not lead you astray.

1 John 4:1 (KJV)

"Beloved, believe not every spirit,
but try the spirits whether they are of God:
because many false prophets are gone out into the world."

It is your eyes that need to see, your ears that need to hear, and your heart that needs to soften and allow Him to work in you, through you, and as you. Developing a relationship with the Godhead is a lifetime's work—one that each of us must complete for ourselves. He knows what is blocking you from Him. He sees your confusion and your doubts. He knows your fear, and He will never give up on you. He loves you. As long as you draw breath, He will do everything in His power to do His part in developing that loving relationship with you. Have faith in the goodness of the Lord.

1 Corinthians 2:5 (KJV)

"That your faith should not stand
in the wisdom of men,
but in the power of God."

This does not mean we should not look to the scriptures, to modern-day prophets, religions, or to others for guidance, inspiration, and wisdom. They are excellent channels for God's wisdom. God will often speak to us and give us revelation through the words of others (ears), their beautiful examples of Christlike living (eyes)—or their heartfelt testimonies (heart).

Churches offer doctrine and rules that, although made by man and imperfect, offer a soul a good framework to grow within, and also good guidelines to protect man from himself. Attending church regularly has been instrumental in developing my personal relationship with God. As man is imperfect, oftentimes his approach to spiritual growth is imperfect, and can benefit from guidance. Again, nothing is a substitute to true understanding and revelation through the guidance of the Holy Spirit, but God uses religion to help guide us as well.

I am humbled by and grateful for the guidance I have received through others. Their mouths, His words. The love in their hearts shared is such a gift. They are wonderful people, who mean well, and want to help, and I'm deeply grateful for each and every one of them. God is also developing a relationship with them as well in accordance with His will and plan for them.

We need to earnestly ask, seek, and knock and put ourselves in the position to receive, find, and have the appropriate doors opened unto us. We need to do our part to come unto God and prepare ourselves to receive His guidance and to develop that relationship with Him personally.

Matthew 13:15 (KJV)

"For this people's heart is waxed gross,
and their ears are dull of hearing,
and their eyes they have closed;
lest at any time they should see with their eyes,
and hear with their ears,
and should understand with their heart,
and should be converted,
and I should heal them."

A significant part of laying down our burdens is setting aside the things within us that block us from receiving promptings and guidance from the Holy Spirit—to set aside the bondages of the natural man and begin to see with spiritual eyes, hear with spiritual ears, and feel with a spiritual heart; the kingdom of heaven that is within us.

Luke 17:20–21 (KJV)

"The kingdom of God cometh not with observation:
Neither shall they say, Lo here! or, lo there!
for, behold, the kingdom of God is within you."

We need to be willing to set aside everything we think we know to be true about God's will, plan, and timing, so that we might allow a better and truer understanding of Him to develop.

We must come to rely upon our relationship with God, having faith that He will add the correct meaning and understanding to external stimuli. Sometimes it is not what is heard, seen, or felt, but how our Heavenly Father wants us to understand it, as He uses words, examples, and testimonies to shape us into who He would have us be—in accordance with His will, His plan, and His timing for us.

I like to think of it as spiritual subtitles accompanying every experience in life. Beyond the surface-level event, there is a message meant for us—and only us. I believe He does this for everyone, drawing from an infinite number of sources. I have seen what I needed to see on a billboard, heard what I needed to hear in a song, and felt what I needed to feel in the beauty of a sunrise. He uses it all to shape us if we are ready and prepared to receive it.

That is why developing a personal relationship with Him is so important: the message is deeply personal, designed specifically for us to understand when we are ready. Many messages from

God can only be discerned spiritually. I believe salvation to be a deeply personal act—between a loving Father and His child. His Spirit to our spirit.

1 Corinthians 2:14 (KJV)

"But the natural man receiveth not the things of the Spirit of God:
for they are foolishness unto him:
neither can he know them,
because they are spiritually discerned."

Core Burden: Resentment toward God

I would like to share with you my path toward God, because it is an example of how I came to misunderstand Him and how I was led astray. For much of my life, I carried resentment toward God and toward the churches of the world.

Growing up was confusing. I saw the hypocrisy of man—people preaching one thing while their actions contradicted their words, their beliefs, and their faith.

With one hand, they spoke of peace, joy, and love; with the other, they divided us from one another because we did not believe exactly the same things.

I saw fear in people—fear that demanded validation, fear that needed to be right and justified in belief. I watched men condemn their brothers and sisters for believing differently, telling them that their God-given understandings were wrong and should not be permitted.

Wars were fought. Atrocities committed. Our human family was divided and scattered about, doing it all in the name of God.

Psalm 10:1 (KJV)

"Why, Lord, do You stand far off?
Why do You hide Yourself in times of trouble?"

As a child, without worldly experience or wisdom, not knowing right from wrong, and without a personal relationship with God, it was difficult not to fear Him and His wrath.

I did not yet understand the difference between God and the actions of men. Because of that, I turned away from Him. I blamed God for the fearful and misguided actions of some of His children. I blamed Him for churches and institutions that divided people in the name of being right.

Psalm 22:1 (KJV)

"My God, my God, why hast Thou forsaken me?
why art Thou so far from helping me,
and from the words of my roaring?"

There were dark times in my life when I felt completely alone, when it seemed there would be no end to my sadness. I wondered where the God was that my parents had compelled me to believe in. I questioned whether He cared for me at all, or whether I meant anything to Him. I could not reconcile the idea of a loving Father with the pain I was experiencing.

Psalm 69:3 (KJV)

"I am weary of my crying:
my throat is dried:
mine eyes fail while I wait for my God."

I endured things no child should have to endure—being assaulted, being molested, being introduced to drugs at a young age by people I trusted.

I struggled with alcoholism and witnessed the damage it caused in my life and in what I lost because of it.

Psalm 61:1–2 (KJV)

"Hear my cry, O God;
attend unto my prayer.
From the end of the earth will I cry unto Thee,
when my heart is overwhelmed:
lead me to the rock that is higher than I."

I watched my three older brothers suffer. As a child, I could not understand that some of their experiences were meant to help shape them. I only saw their pain. I did not want them to be afraid or to feel alone. What I perceived did not look like love to me, and in my ignorance, I blamed God and the church.

Psalm 130:1 (KJV)

"Out of the depths have I cried unto Thee, O LORD."

My brothers struggled with their faith as well, and that strengthened my own resentment. I wanted their acceptance and their love, and I followed them in turning away from God.

Looking back, I see that my anger and contempt were not rightly justified. When I reflect on how I turned my back on Him, how I rebuked Him, the things that I said in anger toward Him, my heart breaks. I have asked for His forgiveness, and He has given it freely, though writing about this still brings me pain.

1 John 1:9 (KJV)

"If we confess our sins,
He is faithful and just to forgive us our sins,
and to cleanse us from all unrighteousness."

As I write this, I wrestle with what I believe to be true. This Core Burden challenges years of loving counsel—rules meant to protect me, covenants meant to guide me, and doctrines meant to enlighten me.

The people who offered that counsel truly loved me. They shared wisdom shaped by their experiences and their personal relationships with God. They wanted me to feel the peace and happiness they had found. Their motives were sincere and good and loving.

But their loving insistence that I believe solely by faith and take their word for it, while ignoring my lived experiences, unanswered questions, and all the evidence of the world, unintentionally pushed me further away and strengthened my resistance to allowing God into my heart.

With time and understanding, as I gained worldly experience and wisdom, I became able to discern right from wrong and began to develop my own relationship with Him.

I came to see that it was not God who caused this suffering. It was the natural man.

As a child, I could not see that distinction because I did not yet understand. But now, as an adult, I do.

I look back on my life now and see the hand of God present in every moment of it. In my darkest hours, He was there—patiently waiting, carrying me when I could not carry myself, comforting me even when I did not want His presence.

When I did not feel His love, it was not because He had withdrawn from me, but because I had closed my heart to Him. And still, He never left. He never gave up on me. He waited. He loved. He endured with me.

John 14:27 (KJV)

"Peace I leave with you, my peace I give unto you:
not as the world giveth, give I unto you.
Let not your heart be troubled,
neither let it be afraid."

The Bible is full of witnesses to God's love for mankind. He is a loving Father, and like any loving Father, He guides His children toward what is good and right. At times, that guidance has required correction—something that can be misunderstood as punishment when viewed without love or context.

I ask the parents reading this: have you ever had to correct one of your children, not out of anger or cruelty, but because you loved them, wanted to protect them, and knew what was best for them even when they could not yet understand it? You know in your heart that the saying is true—that it hurts the parent who corrects more than it hurts the child being corrected.

It pains our Father that we have gone astray. It pains Him that we have turned our backs on Him. He longs for a personal, loving relationship with each and every one of us. All we must do is turn to Him and love Him—He will take care of the rest. He is patiently waiting for us.

Lay down your burdens, the things that separate you from Him. Lay them down; they no longer serve you. You do not need them anymore. Open your heart to Him. Allow Him to breathe into you His peace, His love, and His grace. Allow Him to fill you with the joy that is your birthright. And just as we desire His love, I believe—deeply—that He desires ours as well.

Deuteronomy 6:5 (KJV)

"And thou shalt love the LORD thy God with all thine heart, and with all thy soul, and with all thy might."

CORE BURDEN: PERFECTIONISM

Matthew 5:48 (KJV)

"Be ye therefore perfect, even as your Father which is in heaven is perfect."

For most of my life, I misunderstood this verse. I read it as a direct, personal command—spoken to me alone—that I must become perfect. I heard it as a demand for flawlessness and perfect adherence to Mosaic law: that I must eliminate error, overcome every weakness, and purify myself enough to be acceptable before God. I believed Jesus would not have given this command unless He expected me to achieve it through effort, discipline, and obedience.

Over time, I have come to believe that this interpretation is not only mistaken, but also counterproductive.

The Greek word translated as perfect in Matthew 5:48 is teleios, a word that does not mean flawless or without fault. It means complete or whole. In this light, Jesus is not commanding sinless compliance to the law but pointing toward wholeness—the same wholeness that belongs to the Father.

Scripture consistently uses teleios in this way:

James 1:4

"Let patience have her perfect work, that ye may be perfect and entire, wanting nothing."

Just as importantly, Matthew 5 is not addressed to a single individual striving in isolation. Jesus is speaking to the multitude:

Matthew 5:1–2

"And seeing the multitudes, He went up into a mountain: and when He was set, his disciples came unto Him: and He opened his mouth, and taught them,"

And confirming that He was indeed addressing the multitude;

Matthew 7:28-29

"And it came to pass, when Jesus had ended these sayings, the people were astonished at his doctrine:
For He taught them as one having authority, and not as the scribes."

This matters. The Sermon on the Mount culminates not in a call to private moral flawlessness, but in a vision of communal wholeness rooted in love and trust in God. This echoes Jesus's later prayer:

John 17:21

"That they all may be one; as Thou, Father, art in me, and I in Thee."

Seen this way, Matthew 5:48 is not an impossible demand placed upon the individual soul. It is an invitation to humanity to come together in love, unity, and dependence upon God—mirroring His wholeness rather than striving to be deserving of it.

When Wholeness Is Misunderstood as Flawlessness

When teleios is misread as flawlessness, something subtle but dangerous happens. The soul's longing for wholeness is redirected into a relentless pursuit of self-perfection. What was meant to draw us toward God becomes a burden we place upon ourselves.

This is where perfectionism is born.

At its core, perfectionism is a holy longing misunderstood. The soul remembers oneness—whether consciously or not—and yearns to return to it:

Ecclesiastes 3:11

"He hath set eternity in their heart."

But the human mind, limited and fearful, translates that Eternal longing into a demand for flawlessness. Instead of turning toward God for salvation, we turn inward to self-correction and self-condemnation.

Scripture warns us about this very impulse:

Proverbs 3:5

"Trust in the LORD with all thine heart; and lean not unto thine own understanding."

The heart longs for wholeness. The mind tries to manufacture it.

From Perfectionism to the Law

Once perfectionism takes hold, the next step feels almost inevitable: the law becomes the tool by which we attempt to make ourselves whole.

We begin to believe—often unconsciously—that if we obey enough, repent thoroughly enough, discipline ourselves strictly enough, we can finally become acceptable before God. We begin to relate to God primarily through rules and self-assessment.

Paul speaks directly to this impulse:

Romans 3:20

"Therefore by the deeds of the law there shall no flesh be justified in his sight: for by the law is the knowledge of sin."

The Law of Moses was never given to make humanity whole. It was given to reveal our need and to expose the limits of human effort and self-righteousness. God does not make mistakes. Scripture is clear:

Hebrews 7:19

"For the law made nothing perfect, but the bringing in of a better hope did; by the which we draw nigh unto God."

The law did not fail because it was flawed. It was God given and inspired and as such perfect. It fulfilled its purpose perfectly by proving that obedience alone cannot restore what was broken. His plan being perfect since the beginning of time and in all eternity.

The Old Testament stands as a long, patient witness to this truth: even sincere and disciplined effort cannot make man whole again. Man cannot save man. We cannot fix the problem with the problem.

Paul puts it plainly:

Galatians 3:3

"Are ye so foolish? having begun in the Spirit, are ye now made perfect by the flesh?"

This is not to say that obeying Mosaic Law is not expected or recommended. Personal righteousness still has its place in the preparation of our soul. What I'm saying is that human effort can only shape behavior. Only God can restore wholeness.

The Emotional Cost of Law-Based Perfectionism

When perfectionism drives us toward the law, and the law inevitably exposes our failure, something painful happens inside us. The longing to be whole—once rooted in hope—is transformed into shame.

We do not merely feel that we have failed. We begin to believe we are the failure. We feel like no matter how hard we try; we will eventually come up short.

Shame, born from a lack of perfection, tells us that we are not good enough to be loved, not worthy of forgiveness. We fear rejection. We fear being cast out. We fear that the joy of union with God is for others, but not for us.

This is not the fruit of grace. It is the fruit of misplaced striving. You will know the tree by its fruits.

Scripture describes this tragic exchange:

Romans 10:3 "For they being ignorant of God's righteousness, and going about to establish their own righteousness, have not submitted themselves unto the righteousness of God."

What began as devotion becomes exhaustion and continued failure. What began as a longing to be in His presence again becomes hopelessness. What began as love becomes self-condemnation.

Lay down this burden.

We do not need to be perfect in order to be loved—He already loves us with all that He is. We do not need to be perfect in order to be forgiven—Jesus has already made forgiveness a reality through the Atonement. Because He loves us, and because our sins have already been fully dealt with through Christ, we need not fear His rejection. We are already perfectly lovable exactly as we are. We need not fear being cast out of His presence, for He desires nothing more than to live with us in eternity.

God knew all of this would happen.

Acts 15:18 (KJV)

"Known unto God are all his works from the beginning of the world."

And had a plan to make it all right again.

Romans 8:1–5 (KJV):

"There is therefore now no condemnation to them which are in Christ Jesus, who walk not after the flesh, but after the Spirit.
For the law of the Spirit of life in Christ Jesus hath made me free from the law of sin and death.
For what the law could not do, in that it was weak through the flesh, God sending his own Son in the likeness of sinful flesh, and for sin, condemned sin in the flesh:

That the righteousness of the law might be fulfilled in us, who walk not after the flesh, but after the Spirit."

Your Heavenly Father loves you... He's got you. Now and forever.

And I pray:

"My dearest Heavenly Father, I humbly pray to Thee today,

I ask you to please guide my mind and guide my heart as I walk toward Thee,

I ask Thee to please open my eyes that I might see, and open my ears that I might hear, and soften my heart that I might know You better,

Please Lord allow me to see past my own fears, to see past my own regrets, and shame, and guilt, to see the truth as You would have me understand it.

I'm tired, Lord… I'm tired,

Please hold me and love me and keep me.

Amen."

Chapter 3 - Spiritual Burdens

Sin is not the presence of desire, but the misuse of it. It is the attempt to satisfy a natural, God-given longing with something other than what God has provided—or to pursue fulfillment apart from Him altogether. At its core, sin is the circumvention of holy provision, driven by mistrust in God or by a heart that no longer feels, or refuses to accept, His nearness.

We will not attempt to catalog every sin in this chapter. Instead, I want to explore one in depth—not to dwell on behavior, but to understand what sin is doing beneath the surface, and how it affects our lives in ways we often do not immediately see.

Lust

What follows touches on sensitive subject matter. It is not meant to shame or condemn, but to bring awareness to a burden that harms us and those we love. Freedom begins with honesty. If we are to lay down what weighs upon us, we must first be willing to see it as it truly is.

What follows is an honest look at some of the fruits of lust. You may not identify with all of it—or even any of it. I humbly ask that you remain honest with yourself and keep an open mind. If none of this applies to you personally, there is a strong possibility it applies to someone you know or love.

Before continuing, I invite you to pause. Take a breath. Open your ears, your eyes, and your heart to the Lord. Invite Him into this humbly, with a simple prayer. It need not be grandiose—only sincere.

Prayer:

"God, I love You. Please guide my mind and protect my heart. Allow me to see what You would have me see and feel what You would have me feel, that I might grow closer to You, know You better, and love You more. Please help me, Lord. I trust You. I love You. Amen."

Allow yourself to feel the feelings you need to feel and to think the thoughts you need to think. Do not suppress them. Do not hide from them. Do not censor them. You have invited the Lord into this, and you are in a safe space. There is no judgment here. There is no shame. What we are seeking is honesty and clarity—to see things as they truly are, not as we wish them to be.

I have been influenced, to one degree or another, by this sin and its consequences throughout my life. When I reflect on the ways lust has harmed me and those I love, it pains me deeply.

Lust affects us in two primary ways:

- Our lust harms us and others.
- The lust of others harms us—and themselves.

Matthew 15:18–19 (KJV)
"But those things which proceed out of the mouth come
forth from the heart; and they defile the man.
For out of the heart proceed evil thoughts, murders,
adulteries, fornications, thefts, false witness, blasphemies."

Not all manifestations of lust appear in extreme forms. Many are subtler, quieter, and more socially acceptable. Lust can reside not only in actions, but in attitudes, expectations, glances, comparisons, fantasies, resentments, motives, and unspoken demands.

Lust can create within us an unnaturally excessive need for sex. In an effort to satisfy this need, we may attempt to control our partner. We argue. We tell them they should want more sex, that they should want to please us, that they are failing in their responsibility. We imply—or outright threaten—that if they will not satisfy us, someone else will. Sometimes we threaten to leave. Other times we stay and quietly resent them. Lust introduces shame into a relationship in an attempt to satisfy that which can never truly be satisfied.

We place an impossible burden on our partners, expecting them to meet an insatiable need. We demand that they give what we believe we require because they love us. When they cannot—or will not—we begin to question their love, their commitment, and their integrity. In doing so, we hurt them, often without realizing it. Blinded by our own unmet desires, we become unaware of the suffering our behavior causes.

Lust also harms through distrust. Fueled by unholy fantasies and fear, we assume that because we experience excessive desire, others must as well. We accuse: If you're not getting it from me, you must be getting it from someone else. When driven by fear and unmet desires, we may find ourselves blaming, shaming, arguing, or manipulating without fully realizing what we are doing. At times, this distrust becomes a self-fulfilling prophecy. In our attempts to control, we drive our partner away.

We expect our partners to make us feel whole, loved, wanted, secure, adequate, and important, instead of seeking wholeness in God—knowing that He loves us, trusting that He will not forsake us, knowing that we are children of God.

Children who witness this distorted dynamic are affected as well. In this way, lust becomes a destroyer of families.

When our lustful demands are not met, we may seek satisfaction outside the relationship. Lust sows addictive and destructive behaviors. It leads to pornography addiction. We hide it. We lie. We deceive. When discovered, we may blame our partner, insisting that if they had satisfied us, we would not have turned elsewhere. Pornography profoundly distorts our understanding of sex and intimacy, often leaving lasting damage. Lust leads some to infidelity, prostitution, sex with strangers, and participation in perverse acts—both with others and alone.

Once we have sought to satisfy a God-given desire in a way not aligned with His will, sin—in this case lust—can twist and distort that desire to an extent that is shameful and hurtful, rendering one powerless to control it. This distortion pushes us toward increasingly hedonistic behaviors. It becomes a sinful feedback loop in which the very means we use to satisfy desire make that desire our master. We lose control.

James 1:14–15 (KJV)
"But every man is tempted, when he is drawn away of his own lust, and enticed.
Then when lust hath conceived, it bringeth forth sin: and sin, when it is finished, bringeth forth death."

Often, we find ourselves on the receiving end of lustful behavior. We are the accused—the ones manipulated, cheated on, lied to, and deceived. We are given the impossible task of satisfying an insatiable appetite, exhausting ourselves in futile attempts to quench what cannot be quenched. We continue loving. We want peace. We want our partner to be happy. But the burden placed upon us becomes unbearable.

We see how the constant conflict affects our children, and we realize we must protect them as well. We feel lost and hopeless. We grow angry—not without reason—at the harm being done to us and to our family. When our partner turns to pornography, we feel inadequate, as though we are not enough. When they are unfaithful, our hearts are shattered. Over time, we grow weary. We withdraw. We give up. And eventually, we leave.

Malachi 2:14 (KJV)
"The LORD hath been witness between thee and the wife of thy youth, against whom thou hast dealt treacherously: yet is she thy companion, and the wife of thy covenant."

There are also inward symptoms. Lustful thoughts and fantasies distort what is naturally good. Perverted thoughts, rehearsed again and again, slowly warp the mind and corrupt the heart. For we become what we think about most.

Proverbs 23:7 (KJV)
"For as he thinketh in his heart, so is he."

Lust can also lead us to entertain unholy thoughts about our brothers and sisters without their consent, harming them spiritually. This reality is often misunderstood or minimized, yet its power to divide—to wound communion through inward violation—deserves far greater attention.

Matthew 5:27–28 (KJV)
"Ye have heard that it was said by them of old time, Thou shalt not commit adultery:
But I say unto you, That whosoever looketh on a woman to

lust after her hath committed adultery with her already in his heart."

When we rehearse these unholy methods of satisfying God-given desire in our minds, we strengthen the tendency toward that sin. We add fuel to a fire that eventually consumes us, leaving us powerless to resist—especially when outward opportunity arises. Whether enacted physically or entertained inwardly, sin harms us. Even when no one else is touched, we are.

The purpose of what has been shared here is not to catalog every expression of lust, nor to overwhelm the reader, but to bring awareness, invite honesty, and begin a conversation that leads toward healing and freedom.

I know that many of you have struggled long and hard with lust, as I have. I prayed, fasted, read scripture, sought counsel, made amends—and still fell short. No matter how hard I tried, how many tears I shed, or how earnestly I pleaded, I could not rid myself of lust entirely.

Today, I have a healthier relationship with lust, but I still notice motives that give me pause, and I still catch myself lingering on a sexual thought longer than I wish. What this continues to teach me is that I cannot fix this problem on my own. Because it is tied to such a powerful instinct, it will not disappear overnight.

What I am learning is that lust is a symptom of something much deeper. Beneath it lies a wounded heart, aching to be healed—a fractured heart yearning to be made whole. If we treat only the symptom, the underlying wound will continue to fester.

Sinning doesn't make us horrible people unworthy of His love. Instead of letting Him make us feel loved or happy or adequate, we chose another path. That's it. We chose wrong. We zigged when we should have zagged. It happened. God still loves us.

So hang in there. It will get easier. God loves you, and He is not finished with you. You are not alone in this, and you are not a bad person because you are struggling. Healing takes time, especially when the pain has been carried for a lifetime. Don't give up. This too shall pass.

Core Burden: Pride

What follows is not meant to assign blame or provoke shame. It is simply an attempt to bring awareness to the fruits and burdens of pride. This may feel heavy—but pride is a heavy subject.

Pride separates us from God and from our brothers and sisters, placing us in direct opposition to Christ's two great commandments: to love the Lord our God with all our heart, might, mind, and strength, and to love our neighbor as ourselves. Pride is the great divider.

As you read, do not look for reasons to condemn yourself. This is not an exercise in fault-finding. Scripture tells us that humanity was deceived from the beginning:

Genesis 3:5–6

"For God doth know that in the day ye eat thereof, then your eyes shall be opened, and ye shall be as Gods, knowing good and evil. And when the woman saw that the tree was good for food, and that it was pleasant to the eyes, and a tree to be desired to make one wise, she took of the fruit thereof, and did eat, and gave also unto her husband with her; and he did eat."

Eve's desire to be as God—to define good and evil for herself—outweighed her desire to remain obedient to God and to rely upon Him for all things. This is pride. Pride preceded all sin.

All we can do is become willing to see clearly, to tell the truth about what is happening within us, and to do what we can do to make it right. There is no need to fear what comes next. Pride is not without a remedy. There is a way forward—and we will turn to that together.

Augustine taught that pride is the beginning and mother of all sin—not because every sin feels prideful, but because pride names the posture of the heart that turns away from God and toward the self. Pride begins when the heart stops receiving from God and begins relying on itself. What follows is not a catalog of behaviors, but an exploration of that inward turning: the ways pride speaks, distorts, and separates.

Proverbs 16:18

"Pride goeth before destruction, and a haughty spirit before a fall."

What follows is what pride sounds like when it begins to speak within us.

Pride tells us that all the blessings of our lives were of our own making—that because we performed well, we reaped the benefits of our actions. Pride says the glory and credit for our successes belong to us alone. It tells us we are self-made. It takes credit for all the times our Heavenly Father intervened and carried us. Pride makes us forget the times He guided us, inspired us, protected us, and loved us.

Pride convinces us that our lives are ours to do with as we please, that the only responsibilities we have are to ourselves. Pride ultimately tells us that we do not need God, or even more harmful, that we are God.

Deuteronomy 8:17–18

"And thou say in thine heart, my power and the might of mine hand hath gotten me this wealth. But thou shalt remember the LORD thy God: for it is He that giveth thee power."

Pride makes us forget everyone who helped us along the way. It makes us forget those who loved us, sacrificed for us, believed in us, and supported us when we could not support ourselves. Pride separates us from our brothers and sisters by strengthening the selfishness of the ego. It puffs us up and exalts us beyond our deserved station, leaving us isolated, disconnected, and alone.

Proverbs 13:10 "Only by pride cometh contention."

Pride tells us that we don't need anyone else—that we are self-sufficient, that we can handle anything life throws at us on our own. Pride tells us that reliance on anyone for anything—especially God—is a sign of weakness. It repeats the mantra: If it is to be, then it is up to me. Pride tells us, I got this. I got this. I got this. I, alone.

Jeremiah 17:5

"Thus saith the LORD; Cursed be the man that trusteth in man, and maketh flesh his arm, and whose heart departeth from the LORD."

Pride tells us we will believe only once God gives us a clear revelation. Pride tells us we can be perfect in this mortal life. It tells us we can become whole and complete again without the help of God. Pride tells us we don't need to repent; we just need to do better next time.

Pride tells us we don't need the example of Jesus Christ. Pride tells us we don't need the counsel of the Holy Spirit. Pride tells us we don't need God's grace—and if we do, we can surely earn it on our own.

Ephesians 2:8–9

"For by grace are ye saved through faith; and that not of yourselves: it is the gift of God: not of works, lest any man should boast."

Pride tells us that we have moral authority over others—that we are better than they are, more deserving than they are, more worthy than they are, and more favored than they are. Pride tells us we should be treated differently, with respect and admiration.

Pride tells us that because we work hard and are successful, we can sin with impunity. Pride tells us that the suffering people experience is their burden alone to carry—or that it is God's responsibility, not ours.

James 4:6

"God resisteth the proud, but giveth grace unto the humble."

Pride makes us boast—boasting being an overcompensation for insecurity. It makes us feel good about ourselves when deep down inside we feel unlovable, unworthy, and inadequate.

Pride promises strength but delivers loneliness. Pride is ugly. Pride is unloving. Pride is cold. Pride is suffering.

Proverbs 27:2

"Let another man praise thee, and not thine own mouth."

Pride tells us that we must put up a facade and keep it up—that if we were truly known, we would be rejected; that if the world truly knew us, we would surely fail. Pride tells us we need to show people what they want to see.

Pride tells us we need to be recognized for our good works. Pride tells us we need to tell people that we prayed for them, that we fast often, that we watch sermons, that we are spiritually advanced. Pride tells us we need to prove that we are morally superior.

Matthew 6:1

"Take heed that ye do not your alms before men, to be seen of them."

Pride tells us that we are never wrong—that if we admit fault we will somehow diminish ourselves. Pride tells us that if we apologize, it will mean we owe someone something or give them power over us.

Proverbs 28:13

"He that covereth his sins shall not prosper: but whoso confesseth and forsaketh them shall have mercy."

Pride tells us that once we're perfect, then we can begin our ministry—that we must be complete before we can be useful and helpful.

2 Corinthians 3:5

"Not that we are sufficient of ourselves to think any thing as of ourselves; but our sufficiency is of God."

Pride tells us that if we offer our help to others, they might require too much of us. Pride tells us that if we surrender our will to God, we might not like how He uses us.

Pride tells us that we must be perfect to be loved by God.

Pride deceives. It distorts and twists reality to continually reinforce the belief that we do not need God—that we do not need the example or teachings of Christ, and that we do not need the guidance of the Holy Spirit. Pride tells us that the kingdom of heaven within us is of our own creation, and that any power we possess is also of our own making. Pride tells us we don't need help.

Pride tells us we don't need love.

Pride separates us from our brothers and sisters.
Pride separates us from our Heavenly Father.

Isaiah 59:2

"Your iniquities have separated between you and your God."

Humility: The Way of Christ

What follows is not meant to diminish us or deny our worth. It is an invitation to recognize the fruits and freedom of humility. Humility is not weakness; it is healing. Where pride divides, humility heals—restoring a harmonious relationship with God and with one another, in accordance with Christ's two great commandments: to love the Lord our God with all our heart, might, mind, and strength, and to love our neighbor as ourselves.

Pride turns the soul inward; humility turns it outward toward others and upward toward God.

Philippians 2:5–8

Let this mind be in you, which was also in Christ Jesus:
Who, being in the form of God, thought it not robbery to be equal with God:
But made himself of no reputation, and took upon Him the form of a servant, and was made in the likeness of men:
And being found in fashion as a man, He humbled himself, and became obedient unto death, even the death of the cross.

Christ remained obedient to and reliant upon God in all things—even through the agony of the Garden of Gethsemane, torture, and crucifixion. This was the greatest act of humility in the history of the world.

Augustine taught that humility is the foundation of every virtue because it keeps the heart and mind rightly oriented toward God. Where pride claims ownership, humility remembers gift. Where pride divides, humility unites.

What follows is what humility sounds like when it begins to speak within us.

Humility tells us that our blessings are gifts from God—that we do not own them, but are merely stewards meant to multiply them by giving them away, just as they were freely given to us.

Humility teaches gratitude: for every moment, every heartbeat, every breath. It calls us to remember the times that were dark and overwhelming, when we were outmatched and God intervened—comforting us, carrying us, guiding us.

Humility is a living remembrance in the heart of all the love He has given us, all the inspiration, guidance, and light.

1 Corinthians 4:7

"What hast thou that thou didst not receive?"

Humility tells us that we are not alone—that we are part of something far greater than ourselves. It reminds us that the needs of mankind and creation are not separate from our own but intertwined with them.

Humility tells us that we are all children of a loving God, and it keeps present in our minds and hearts those who helped us along our path—those who loved us, sacrificed for us, believed in us, and supported us when, without them, we would have fallen.

Romans 12:4–5

"For as we have many members in one body, and all members have not the same office:
So we, being many, are one body in Christ, and every one members one of another."

Humility strengthens our relationship with our brothers and sisters by keeping the ego in check. It helps us maintain a proper standing among others, welcoming union, connection, and togetherness. It teaches us that together we are greater than the sum of our parts, and that together we can accomplish far more than we ever could alone. It tells us that it is okay to receive help—both from one another, and especially from God.

Galatians 6:2

"Bear ye one another's burdens, and so fulfil the law of Christ."

Humility teaches us that God can work great wonders through us—His glory, His power, His plan. It tells us that it is a blessing and an honor to be instruments of His light, love, and peace in the world—His will, our hands. Humility tells us that together we can endure and overcome the trials and tribulations of life.

2 Corinthians 4:7

"But we have this treasure in earthen vessels, that the excellency of the power may be of God, and not of us."

Humility helps us see the needs of others, to care for their well-being, and to place their needs before our own, because it allows us to see others as God sees them—as perfectly lovable miracles of creation. When we recognize suffering in the life of another, humility invites us to respond with love and compassion, and when possible, to offer help. We cannot solve every problem, but we can always choose to love.

Philippians 2:4

"Look not every man on his own things, but every man also on the things of others."

Humility allows us to feel the unconditional love of God and to receive love from our brothers and sisters. It tells us that we are worthy of love and of blessings—that we are exactly as we are meant to be in this moment.

Humility allows God to turn weakness into strength. It makes it safe to make mistakes, reconciles us with imperfection, and gives us genuine compassion for ourselves.

Humility allows patience with ourselves and trust that, in time, we will become who God would have us become and live the life He would have us live.

2 Corinthians 12:9

"My strength is made perfect in weakness."

Humility is beautiful. Humility is love. Humility is a warming embrace. It gives us the courage to be ourselves and to let the world see us as we truly are. It gives us the courage to be vulnerable, knowing that our vulnerability gives others permission to be vulnerable as well. Humility pulls down the walls we built to keep ourselves safe—walls that became prisons.

Humility allows us to pray for others without expectation, to love without the need for reciprocation, and to celebrate the success of others without envy or jealousy—simply rejoicing because we love them. Humility teaches us to trust God's plan and purpose for us, giving us the courage to serve now, even when we feel unready, trusting that God will make us ready.

Philippians 1:6

"Being confident of this very thing, that He which hath begun a good work in you will perform it."

Humility teaches us that through daily repentance we willingly open our hearts to God, allowing Him to forgive us our sins and to remove whatever separates us from Him, from one another, and from the fullness of the life He desires to give us.

Humility draws us toward Jesus Christ, stirring a desire to know Him more deeply, to become more like Him, and to love Him as He loves us.

Humility teaches us to cherish the gift of the Holy Spirit—loving it, nurturing it, appreciating it, and delighting in it.

Humility helps us to align our will and our lives with His.

Matthew 11:29

"Learn of me; for I am meek and lowly in heart."

Humility allows us to know the love of God now—in this moment, and in every moment—not in some distant afterlife or after we become perfect. Humility enlightens. It opens our minds and hearts so we can continue to learn and grow.

Humility allows us to see God's hand in all creation and in our lives and the lives of those we love. Humility unites us with our brothers and sisters in love. Humility unites us with God in love.

John 17:21

"That they all may be one."

I hope this section has shed light on pride and on God's answer to it: humility. My hope is that something you have read here has softened your heart, creating space for God to work in you, through you, and as you, in deeper and more beautiful ways than you can ever understand. Perhaps it has revealed places where you have turned away from Him—sometimes knowingly, but more often without realizing it. We have all been deceived at times.

God does not shame us or condemn us. As I have said throughout this book, our Heavenly Father loves us. He desires to be part of our lives now, and He longs, above all else, to draw us home—to be reunited with us in eternity.

Core Burden: Self-Reliance — Seeking Wholeness Apart from God

We attempt to heal a rupture between ourselves and God using external, temporal measures. The separation introduced by the fall is eternal and relational in nature, yet we reach for what is immediate and impermanent to repair it. We try to fix what is eternal with what is temporal—a task that can never succeed. At best, these attachments offer brief relief; at worst, they deepen the sense of lack. What the soul longs for cannot be satisfied by what was never meant to endure.

First, let us examine the eternity we are attempting to repair with the temporal.

The Fall — A Departure from Wholeness

In Genesis 3, we are given more than an account of deception, disobedience, and punishment; we are shown the anatomy of the Fall. The serpent does not begin by tempting behavior, but by planting doubt: Did God really say that we would die if we ate from the tree of the knowledge of good and evil? The separation between humanity and God—and the beginning of God's response to it, the Plan of Salvation—begins with deception, leads to doubt, and is finalized in desire: desire for food and the prideful desire to be as God.

Genesis 3:4–5 (KJV)

"And the serpent said unto the woman, ye shall not surely die: For God doth know that in the day ye eat thereof, then your eyes shall be opened, and ye shall be as Gods, knowing good and evil."

Pride follows quickly. The promise offered is exaltation: You will be like God. In the Garden of Eden, humanity walked with

God. He was always present. We were one with Him. He gave us everything we could ever need, including His love. Adam was His child, and God gave Adam a boundary meant to protect him from himself and preserve the perfection they enjoyed together.

Genesis 2:16–17 (KJV)

"And the LORD God commanded the man, saying, Of every tree of the garden thou mayest freely eat:
But of the tree of the knowledge of good and evil, thou shalt not eat of it: for in the day that thou eatest thereof thou shalt surely die."

The moment the fruit is eaten, something is broken.

Genesis 3:6 (KJV)

"And when the woman saw that the tree was good for food, and that it was pleasant to the eyes, and a tree to be desired to make one wise, she took of the fruit thereof, and did eat, and gave also unto her husband with her; and he did eat."

They become aware of their nakedness—not merely physical exposure, but vulnerability, lack, and apartness. Immediately, humanity reaches for a solution. Fig leaves are sewn together. Hiding follows. Blame is assigned. This is our first example of attempting to fix an eternal rupture with something temporal.

Genesis 3:7 (KJV)

"And the eyes of them both were opened, and they knew that they were naked; and they sewed fig leaves together, and made themselves aprons."

The fig leaves only covered the body; they did not heal the schism between humanity and God. They merely hid shame, guilt, and regret. Knowing something was wrong, Adam and Eve hid themselves from God among the trees of the garden.

Genesis 3:8 (KJV)

"And they heard the voice of the LORD God walking in the garden in the cool of the day: and Adam and his wife hid themselves from the presence of the LORD God amongst the trees of the garden."

God had expressly stated the law that was not to be broken and clearly communicated the consequence: death. By choosing to break the law and eat the fruit, Adam and Eve did, in fact, choose death.

Genesis 3:22–24 (KJV)

"And the LORD God said, Behold, the man is become as one of us, to know good and evil: and now, lest he put forth his hand, and take also of the tree of life, and eat, and live for ever: Therefore the LORD God sent him forth from the garden of Eden, to till the ground from whence he was taken. So He drove out the man; and He placed at the east of the garden of Eden Cherubims, and a flaming sword which turned every way, to keep the way of the tree of life."

This was not punishment—it was protection. Protection from eternal corruption, had they eaten from the Tree of Life, rooted in an imperfect nature.

Deuteronomy 32:4 (KJV)

"He is the Rock, his work is perfect: for all his ways are judgment: a God of truth and without iniquity, just and right is He."

Numbers 23:19 (KJV)

"God is not a man, that He should lie; neither the son of man, that He should repent: hath He said, and shall He not do it? or hath He spoken, and shall He not make it good?"

There must be law, or there is no sin.
There must be sin, or there is no occasion for justice.
There must be justice, or God would cease to be God.
Therefore, mercy must fulfill justice—not deny it.

God did not abandon His children. He prepared them for their journey home.

Genesis 3:21 (KJV)

"Unto Adam also and to his wife did the LORD God make coats of skins, and clothed them."

Mortality — Our Journey Home Begins

Adam and Eve stood suddenly without covering, without assured provision, and without the immediate presence of God as they had known it. The communion that once made them whole, secure, and at rest was no longer experienced in the same way. In its absence, fear entered. Exposure followed. Humanity, once at ease in the presence of God, now hid from Him.

Scripture does not tell us what Adam and Eve felt in full detail, but the narrative suggests confusion and sorrow. Why would a loving Father allow exile? How could a world now marked by pain, toil, and death be an expression of love? Whatever their internal experience, the external reality was clear: life would now be lived east of Eden.

Forced to live life on life's terms, without the immediate assurance of God's presence, humanity began to adapt. Man learned to seek security, comfort, meaning, and provision from what was now available—the temporal world. What began as survival gradually became substitution: seeking in creation what had once been received freely through communion with the Creator.

Within the human soul, there now existed a void—a space once filled by the presence of a loving God. Humanity set out into the wilderness seeking a way back, seeking to heal the soul, seeking to fill that absence. With only limited understanding, we reached for what we had: our actions, our thoughts, our emotions, and the imperfect world into which we had been exiled.

At the time of exile, God did not abandon His children. He clothed them. He protected them from eternal corruption by barring access to the Tree of Life. Yet no full plan was yet revealed—no Law to guide conduct, no detailed path explaining how the rupture between God and humanity would one day be healed. Life would now involve thorns and thistles, labor and fatigue, sustenance earned by sweaty effort until death returned man to the ground.

Genesis 3:17–19 (KJV)

"Cursed is the ground for thy sake; in sorrow shalt thou eat of it all the days of thy life;
Thorns also and thistles shall it bring forth to thee; and thou shalt eat the herb of the field;
In the sweat of thy face shalt thou eat bread, till thou return unto the ground."

God, like a loving Father, revealed truth progressively, according to humanity's capacity to receive it. In time, He gave the Law—to restrain sin and teach righteousness. Later, He gave hope fully revealed through Jesus Christ: remission of sins through the Atonement and direction through the two great commandments—to love God wholly and to love one's neighbor as oneself.

Self-reliance began as necessity but slowly hardened into identity. Humanity needed food, shelter, companionship, safety, and meaning—things once freely provided in Eden. What was required to endure life in a fallen world quietly became a substitute for reliance upon God.

We attempted to fill the void within us with things of the world. We sought companionship to heal loneliness, mistaking union with another human being for wholeness. We used ambition and labor to secure provision, replacing the total dependence once enjoyed in Eden. We turned to entertainment, sex, food, drink, and substances in an attempt to recreate comfort, rest, and peace. We pursued success and achievement to manufacture purpose and meaning, substituting our own plans for God's will.

With limited understanding, we did what we could. Our ignorance explains our striving—but it does not make us whole.

Everything changes once God reveals His plan for redemption. The Law exposes sin but cannot remove it. Christ fulfills the Law and offers reconciliation through grace. Faith in Him, obedience born of love, and reliance upon His grace—not our own strength—become the path back to wholeness.

Hebrews 10:19–22 (KJV)

"Having therefore, brethren, boldness to enter into the holiest by the blood of Jesus, By a new and living way, which He hath consecrated for us, through the veil, that is to say, his flesh; And having an high priest over the house of God; Let us draw near with a true heart in full assurance of faith, having our hearts sprinkled from an evil conscience, and our bodies washed with pure water."

This is why self-reliance must be laid down. We need God for us to become whole again. We need Him for resurrection, for eternal life, and for restoration. An Eternal rupture cannot be healed by temporal means. We cannot fix the problem with the problem. We cannot lift ourselves back to God by our own effort.

Proverbs 3:5–6 (KJV)

"Trust in the LORD with all thine heart; and lean not unto thine own understanding.
In all thy ways acknowledge Him, and He shall direct thy paths."

Self-reliance becomes a trap when it attempts to replace God rather than submit to Him. It convinces us that because life appears good—because we are productive, successful, generous, loved, and moral—we must be whole. It dulls our awareness of the deeper loss, the original separation we have spent our lives compensating for.

Jeremiah 17:5–8 (KJV)

"Thus saith the LORD; Cursed be the man that trusteth in man, and maketh flesh his arm, and whose heart departeth from the LORD.

For he shall be like the heath in the desert, and shall not see when good cometh; but shall inhabit the parched places in the wilderness, in a salt land and not inhabited.

Blessed is the man that trusteth in the LORD, and whose hope the LORD is.

For he shall be as a tree planted by the waters, and that spreadeth out her roots by the river, and shall not see when heat cometh, but her leaf shall be green; and shall not be careful in the year of drought, neither shall cease from yielding fruit."

We forget the fear and exposure of Eden's exile because we have learned to live with the ache. We have filled the void with people, places, and things. Yet the patchwork always fails. What the soul longs for—peace, joy, unconditional love, and grace—can only be received through reliance upon God and faith in His plan of salvation.

Romans 10:1–4 (KJV)

"Brethren, my heart's desire and prayer to God for Israel is, that they might be saved.
For I bear them record that they have a zeal of God, but not according to knowledge.
For they being ignorant of God's righteousness, and going about to establish their own righteousness, have not submitted themselves unto the righteousness of God.
For Christ is the end of the law for righteousness to everyone that believeth."

Where Self-Reliance Fails Us

Proverbs 14:12 (KJV)

"There is a way which seemeth right unto a man, but the end thereof are the ways of death."

Self-reliance, as good as it is and as wonderful the fruits that it can produce in the form of material things, has one fatal flaw: it is of man, and as such is imperfect, impermanent, and fleeting.

We sow seeds of success and achievement through hard work, determination, struggle, and toil—oftentimes through courageous, disciplined, and magnificent efforts—yet reap fruit that can always be taken away from us. Fruit that we can lose. Fruit that can fail us.

Loved ones pass away.
Marriages are broken.
Jobs and careers are lost.
Personal belongings break and can be stolen.
Homes are taken from us through disaster.
We are afflicted with all manner of disease.
Our bodies fail us.
Financial institutions fail.
People let us down and betray us—
and on and on and on.

Nothing in this world ever lasts. Nothing.

And we know this. Deep down inside, we know this to be true.

We rush out with all of our energy, attempting to prevent loss, attempting to prevent suffering, attempting to prevent death. It's exhausting, as it is a continual fight for the things we have and for the things we don't have that we think we need. We are always on alert, never being able to truly rest.

Relentlessly, we are driven by an insatiable need to feel safe, to feel loved, to feel whole—but never being able to truly find it. As we see that the fruits of our labors are always in danger of being taken from us, we redouble our efforts and our will. We try harder, grasping and clawing and doing everything we can do to hold onto those things that have brought us comfort, a false sense of security, conditional love, and our place in society.

Matthew 6:19–21 (KJV)

"Lay not up for yourselves treasures upon earth, where moth and rust doth corrupt, and where thieves break through and steal:
But lay up for yourselves treasures in heaven, where neither moth nor rust doth corrupt, and where thieves do not break through nor steal:
For where your treasure is, there will your heart be also."

There is this underlying anxiety and fear, distorting and twisting our God-given instincts, birthing all manner of sins into our lives.

Sex makes us feel good, so we grasp for more of that.
Lust.

Food makes us feel good, so we consume more than we could ever possibly need.
Gluttony.

Possessions give us a sense of security, so we hoard as much as we can, keeping everything we can for ourselves.
Greed.

We covet the possessions, spouses, and jobs of others and turn our relentless need for wholeness toward acquiring them for ourselves.
Envy. Jealousy. Covetousness.

We see, too, that other people have an eye for the things we hold dear as well, and we resent and despise them for it.
Hate.

Exhausted from all this effort—this constant striving and protection, the constant need to produce—we seek withdrawal from it, as it can become too much.
Sloth.

And maybe we find something that is really good at giving us comfort, or sex, or rest, or peace of mind, and we become addicted to it. Our need is so powerful that we bow down to it and lose all control. Our deep neediness for all things makes them our master.

Something imperfect cannot create something that is perfect.

Self-reliance is a corrupt tree, being flawed and impermanent, and brings forth flawed and impermanent fruit. We are broken creatures, fractured at our core—a God-sized void in our heart that can never be filled, no matter how many things we pour into it.

There is nothing we can do about it.
It is beyond all human power.

We will feel loss.
We will suffer.
We will die.

Self-reliance is a futile and oftentimes unnecessarily painful attempt at redemption and salvation—a desperate attempt to stave off the inevitable.

Matthew 7:16–20 (KJV)

"Ye shall know them by their fruits. Do men gather grapes of thorns, or figs of thistles?
Even so every good tree bringeth forth good fruit; but a corrupt tree bringeth forth evil fruit.
A good tree cannot bring forth evil fruit, neither can a corrupt tree bring forth good fruit.
Every tree that bringeth not forth good fruit is hewn down, and cast into the fire.
Wherefore by their fruits ye shall know them."

Where Reliance on God Blesses Us

Matthew 11:28–30 (KJV)
"Come unto me, all ye that labour and are heavy laden, and I will give you rest.
Take my yoke upon you, and learn of me; for I am meek and lowly in heart: and ye shall find rest unto your souls.
For my yoke is easy, and my burden is light."

The problem, as we've seen, with self-reliance is that it rests on things that can be lost or taken from us—things that will break, things that will fade away, things that inevitably lead to pain, suffering, insecurity, and fear. Its foundation is impermanent, imperfect, and unreliable. As we have seen in our discussion of self-reliance, it not only fails to solve the most important question of all—How do I become whole again in eternity with God?—it also fails to give us lasting happiness in our day-to-day life. Self-reliance is the way of pain, anxiety, and fear.

Reliance upon God not only solves the most important question—How do I become whole in eternity?—it also gives us blessings that cannot be taken away, blessings that, when given away, are not diminished but multiplied. I am not talking about blessings of cars, promotions, homes, relationships, or possessions, although those things may come as a byproduct of receiving the true blessings that are of God.

Love—true, Eternal, lasting, unconditional, and perfect love. A love that comes from within us and is a choice we can make in any moment, no matter how dark or perilous that moment may be. We can always choose to act in love. It is a connection with others that transcends personalities, transcends situations, and transcends time and distance, and it is the antidote for the ailments of humanity. It is why His two great commandments are to love Him with all that we are and to love our neighbor as ourselves.

Serenity—an indescribable sense of peace and well-being born of acceptance and surrender; an unwavering calm that helps us endure the difficult moments of life. Through serenity, we can accept others exactly as they are in this moment. We recognize that God has a plan for them, and that they are both God's responsibility and their own. Serenity allows us to see that if we had lived all the moments they have lived, endured all the pain they have endured, we might act in the very same way.

Joy—a magnificent and powerful sense of contentment born of gratitude for all the moments of our lives, both good and bad. Born from gratitude for the knowledge that He has always been with us and always will be. Born from a deep knowing that He loves us with all that He is. Joy flows from the understanding that every moment of our lives—pleasant or painful—has been part of His design to shape us into the people we need to become to live the lives He has prepared for us. That all things have been guiding us back toward an eternity of love and oneness with Him. This, too, shall pass. Life is a celebration.

Acceptance—a component of serenity, but also a blessing in and of itself—allows us to see that people are exactly as they are meant to be in this moment. It gives rise to compassion rather than judgment. It allows us to live life on life's terms, not evading life or hiding from it, but meeting whatever comes without losing our peace or becoming someone we will later regret. We no longer have to fight every battle, fix every problem, or carry responsibility for everything. Through acceptance, we find serenity and true rest.

Hope—a deep assurance that everything will ultimately be okay, no matter how uncertain the present moment feels. Though we do not know how things will unfold, through the Atonement of Christ we trust that they will culminate in eternity with Him. Hope strengthens us in dark seasons, fortifying us with integrity and quiet joy. It steadies us when life feels as though it is happening to us, granting peace of mind and steadfastness of spirit. Hope is the light that dispels doubt, insecurity, and anxiety. It enables us to face life's trials with gratitude and to become a source of light for others walking similar paths.

These are but a few of the blessings we receive when we rely on God rather than ourselves. What we receive when we become willing to rely on God is union with Him, a perfect example in Jesus Christ, and a guiding companion in the Holy Spirit. His foundation is Eternal, unwavering, unchangeable, wholly reliable, and cannot be stolen, lost, or damaged.

How do we make the shift from relying on ourselves to relying on God? How do we set aside a lifetime of doing things our way and accept a radically different way of living? The key to living life on God's terms is developing a willingness to surrender our will and our lives to Him, allowing Him to align our will with His so that we may walk the path He has prepared for us. Surrender allows for the alignment of our will—not its destruction. We do not disappear, nor are we diminished. In fact, surrender, as an act of humility, serves only to strengthen us and allows us to be exalted in accordance with His Eternal plan for humanity.

Matthew 6:33–34 (KJV)
"But seek ye first the kingdom of God, and his righteousness; and all these things shall be added unto you.
Take therefore no thought for the morrow: for the morrow shall take thought for the things of itself. Sufficient unto the day is the evil thereof."

Reliance upon God produces peace, rest, clarity, freedom, strength, and fruit—now, not only in eternity.

Most blessings from God are not temporal, though He may bless us with material things as well. The greater purpose of His blessings is to prepare us for eternity with Him while also increasing the quality of our lives here and now. Man is that he might have joy. We become better husbands and wives, better parents, better friends, better neighbors, and better members of society. As we are transformed inwardly, life naturally reflects that transformation outwardly. We seek God first, He changes us, and the external blessings we once chased follow in their proper order.

Reliance upon God does not guarantee the absence of hardship, but it does enable us to endure hardship well. Difficult seasons, meant to shape us into the likeness of Christ, serve to deepen our love, acceptance, serenity, joy, and hope. They also strengthen something essential that has not yet been fully addressed: faith—faith in the Atonement of Christ as the means by which we are reunited with Him in eternity.

Romans 12:1–2 (KJV)
"I beseech you therefore, brethren, by the mercies of God, that ye present your bodies a living sacrifice, holy, acceptable unto God, which is your reasonable service.
And be not conformed to this world: but be ye transformed by the renewing of your mind, that ye may prove what is that good, and acceptable, and perfect, will of God."

You will not change overnight. These blessings will not arrive all at once. God gives them when we are ready to receive them. What matters most is knowing that God will not forsake you. He will not let you down. All that is required to begin is willingness—simple willingness to surrender your will to Him. Humbly ask for His guidance, seek His wisdom through prayer and scripture, and knock upon the door so that it may be opened to you.

Remember: your Heavenly Father loves you. Everything will be okay.

Matthew 6:25–26 (KJV)
"Therefore I say unto you, Take no thought for your life, what ye shall eat, or what ye shall drink; nor yet for your body, what ye shall put on. Is not the life more than meat, and the body than raiment?
Behold the fowls of the air: for they sow not, neither do they reap, nor gather into barns; yet your heavenly Father feedeth them. Are ye not much better than they?"

My heart has been broken, and it has been healed.
What was lost, has been found.

And I pray:

"Lord, forgive me for I have sinned against Thee. I have turned my back on Thee. I have cursed Thee.

I have been lost, apart from Thee, bereft of Your presence, alone in the wilderness, I have suffered.

I ask Thee Lord to forgive me my trespasses against Thee. I knew not what I did. I was deceived.

I didn't mean it Lord, I'm so very sorry. Words cannot express it, but You know my heart Lord and You see it there.

Life has been so difficult without You. I have struggled, labored, and endured a great many things.

Lord, I see now that You were always there with me, patiently awaiting my call to Thee, that You might comfort me and love me, that I might know that You are indeed my Heavenly Father and that You love me, oh Lord.

I see the error of my ways now. I see them, and I'm sorry.

I see Your Hand in all of it Lord, and I'm grateful for all of it. Good and bad, because it all led me here to this moment with You.

I love You so very much Lord. So very much.

Thank You. Thank You. Thank You.

Amen."

Part Two:
Letting Go

Preparing Ourselves to Lay Down our Burdens

By now, I hope you've begun to recognize the burdens you've been holding onto and how they've been affecting your life and your relationship with God. This isn't about assigning blame; it's about seeing that letting go is now a choice you can make.

Taking responsibility in this way is not about condemnation; it's about empowerment. It means you now have the ability to respond differently and access the strength needed to lay your burdens down. You don't have to carry them anymore or figure everything out on your own.

Part Two and Three are about the states of heart and mind that lead you to the true source of that power—God Himself. The good news is you're not alone, and you don't have to do this by yourself. We can't fix the problem with the problem; we need a power greater than ourselves. That power is God, who created you, loves you, and wants you to find joy and live with Him.

God's healing and restorative power is available to all who seek it. All that's required is a willingness to humble ourselves, admit we've been carrying these burdens, and ask Him to help remove them from our lives.

In Part Four you will be laying them down.

Chapter 4 –Willingness

WILLINGNESS — Opening our hearts to God.

How do we go about asking, seeking, and knocking in a way that invites the loving, healing, purifying presence of God into our lives?

How do we establish a relationship with Him — one that can be nurtured, fed, and allowed to grow?

How do we invite the Spirit of God into our hearts and allow Him to heal us, restore us, and bless us?

How do we receive the gift of the Holy Spirit and learn to accept guidance, inspiration, and comfort from Him?

God does not require perfected obedience, full repentance, complete understanding, or surrender in the beginning — only willingness.

On the night of my last drink, as I mentioned earlier in this book, I lay on my bathroom floor — burning, crying that painful cry that makes no sound, aching, broken, devoid of hope, and utterly alone.

Then, like a blanket, a feeling of complete numbness and safety fell over me. My mind stopped racing. My heart stopped hurting. My body stopped aching. The fear that had tormented me disappeared, and there was complete silence.

Then I heard a voice, clear as day:

"Call your stepmother… Call your stepmother…"

That was the night of my last drink.

Psalm 34:18
"The Lord is near to the brokenhearted
And saves those who are crushed in spirit."

When I spoke with my father, he recommended rehab. Although this meant I might lose my job — and, in turn, my home — I was willing to do whatever it took to lay that burden down. Because if I didn't stop drinking, I would have lost them anyway.

When I arrived at rehab, I wanted nothing to do with God or with Alcoholics Anonymous, which I felt was being forced on me. I just wanted twenty-eight days to turn a drinking habit into a sobriety habit.

I refused group meetings. I refused AA meetings. I was going to do this on my own.

I exercised twice a day. I ate healthy. I read a medical book explaining alcoholism as a purely physical disease. I had everything covered — or so I thought. I was going to make this work by myself.

One November morning, about ten days into rehab, I was running a trail that circled the facility. The path ran alongside a beautiful stream, with benches placed at intervals facing the water. I don't know why I stopped and sat on one of them — but I did.

I became lost in the sound of the stream cascading over river stones — a small, steady rhythm. It was cold. I felt the wetness of the bench against my body. And all I could think about was how tired I was. Tired of living a life that required so much energy and constant struggle.

Then something happened — a moment that will bring tears to my eyes for the rest of my life.

My face soaked with tears that seemed to come from nowhere. I began crying uncontrollably, trembling like a child desperate to be held.

I, a man who didn't need or want God in any way, began to pray.

And that same numbness and safety I had felt on my bathroom floor fell over me again. This time I knew it was God as surely as I knew the sun would rise in the east.

In that moment, I surrendered my life to Him — to do with and build as He saw fit. I was tired of fighting. Tired of needing to be right. Tired of the struggle, the suffering, the broken heart, and the constant anxiety that framed my life.

I was so very tired. My soul is so very weary. I didn't want it anymore.

I asked Him to take it all from me, and I became willing to give myself to Him — root and branch. All of me. He could have all of me.

John 14:16–18 (KJV)
And I will pray the Father, and He shall give you another
Comforter, that He may abide with you for ever;
Even the Spirit of truth; whom the world cannot receive,
because it seeth Him not, neither knoweth Him: but ye know
Him; for He dwelleth with you, and shall be in you.
I will not leave you comfortless: I will come to you.

Looking back on those two moments that redefined my life, I am profoundly grateful for both. What I see now is how I invited God into my life.

On the bathroom floor, beaten into submission by alcoholism, I became willing to do whatever it took to not be that man anymore — to not live that life anymore. I did not choose surrender. I did not turn my life over to God. I merely became willing.

By planting that seed of willingness, something within me began to grow — something that fully unfolded on that bench ten days later.

For a long time, I believed the miracle happened that November morning. Looking back now, I see that it began on the bathroom floor.

That warm presence I felt on that bathroom floor and then again on the bench, was the Holy Spirit. It was His voice I heard that night — and it saved me.

It was not something I did.

It was not something I earned.

It was a taste of grace.

I was broken willing — and that was all He needed.

Isaiah 57:15
"For thus says the High and Lofty One
Who inhabits eternity, whose name is Holy:
I dwell in the high and holy place,
With him who has a contrite and humble spirit,
To revive the spirit of the humble,
And to revive the heart of the contrite ones."

What I hope the first three chapters have done is help you find that same willingness within yourself — the willingness to do whatever it takes to lay your burdens down.

I hope you are now willing to set aside the things within you that have been the source of your suffering and allow the Holy Spirit into your life so He can gently and lovingly show you how.

You don't have to know how yet.

You only have to be willing to let Him in.

And I pray:

"God, I come before Ye humbled by the moments of my life.

I carry the weight of the world on my shoulders, I carry so much pain in my heart, my strength has proven to not be enough, my understanding has proven to be incomplete, my heart is broken, God, and I cannot fix it alone.

I carry these things with me that separate me from Thee and those about me, I carry these things with me that no longer serve me and certainly don't serve You or anyone else.

I ask Thee Lord, if it be Thy will, that You allow me to develop the willingness to let You in, so that You might breath Your love and peace into my soul, that You might relieve me of these burdens that I carry, that I might finally be able to lay them down.

I humbly and meekly ask You for the willingness to set my selfish fearful needs aside that I might learn to love You better and learn to love my brothers and sisters the way You love them. Amen"

Chapter 5 - Acceptance

ACCEPTANCE - Releasing resistance to reality

God uses the circumstances of our lives to shape us, guide us, and direct us. He uses them to keep us on the path He laid out from the beginning of time—a path that leads us toward becoming the creation He intended us to be. Life is a preparatory state, preparing us for reunion with Him in eternity.

Like a great forge, life molds us through heat and force—through God's fire and hammer—shaping us more and more into His likeness. He burns away our imperfections, our doubts, our fears, and our false beliefs—anything that separates us from Him. He hammers out our weaknesses, our pride, and our self-reliance, forming within us the humility necessary to establish a loving relationship with Him.

God uses the circumstances of our lives to mirror back to us the very things we choose, by our own agency, to hold onto—those things He cannot take from us unless we freely give them to Him.

He does not protect us from pain, suffering, or failure; those are often His tools. Rather, He protects us from ourselves and from our human tendency to sow destruction in our own lives.

The pain, suffering, and failure we experience are not attempts to hurt or punish us. They are a system of loving correction—a set of checks and balances that reveal the error of our ways and gently redirect us.

When we choose prideful and selfish paths, we oppose God's will, and our lives become disharmonious. When we choose humility and God's way, we come back into harmony, and our circumstances reflect that alignment.

Life is a feedback loop, always leading us back to Him—either through correction or through surrender. We choose suffering when we fight against God's will and direction. We resist the very situations He uses to guide us, and we feel pain because of that resistance.

What I have come to understand is this: when I chose my way, life responded with disharmonious results. When I chose God's way, life responded with harmonious results. In both cases, the outcomes were never truly mine to control. My actions, my choices, my beliefs—those were mine. The results were His. The circumstances of my life have always been God's direction—Good Orderly Direction.

Ecclesiastes 3:9–11

"What profit hath he that worketh in that wherein he
laboureth?
I have seen the travail, which God hath given to the sons of
men to be exercised in it.
He hath made every thing beautiful in his time: also He hath
set the world in their heart, so that no man can find out the
work that God maketh from the beginning to the end."

As I reflect on my life—both the good times and the bad—I see now that things could not have unfolded any other way. God used addiction and alcoholism to strengthen me and to guide me back to Him. Through those experiences, and through overcoming them only with His help, a witness and testimony was formed within me—one meant to be given away to help others who walk a similar path.

I was molested as a child, and in time I was led to a choice: whether I would remain bound by that harm or choose forgiveness. Through that painful process, I came to understand that even the deepest wounds can be redeemed, and that forgiveness is possible—even when it feels impossible.

When I was sixteen, I was brutally beaten by a group of men. That violence disrupted an unhealthy relationship that had been pulling me toward methamphetamine-driven oblivion. What felt at the time like a senseless act of violence became a means of deliverance.

He molded me into an instrument of His will, His plan, and His timing. He allowed me to suffer so that I might come to the end of myself and finally turn to Him. Yet I was never forsaken. He never once left my side. When I reached the realization that I could not escape on my own power, He stepped in and revealed His love, His grace, and His peace.

Looking back, I no longer see the dark times as punishment, but as loving correction. I no longer see the good times as reward, but as loving confirmation. My life was not a series of mistakes, missed opportunities, disasters, failures, or even successes. It was a series of course corrections—adjustments to my sails—guiding me home.

I accept now that my life could not have been any other way, or it would have been. The pain was necessary. The failure was necessary. The suffering was necessary. None of it was in vain. All of it served my greater good. All of it kept me on the path of fall, repentance, atonement, and Eternal life—working to heal what was broken and make my relationship with God whole again.

Seeing life through this lens changes everything. I now look for God's guidance in adversity and His direction in struggle. In the midst of suffering, I ask how I set the process in motion—how my choices created the conditions that allowed God to redirect me. Pain becomes instruction. Suffering becomes understanding. Adversity becomes a pathway to humility.

I accept that some of the suffering in my life has been self-chosen, born of my free will and even my best intentions. By accepting life on life's terms—my way leading to disharmony, God's way to harmony—I find rest in His will. I no longer fight current circumstances. I accept that what is happening must happen, and I welcome His guidance, inspiration, and love.

I no longer try to control outcomes. I see now that I never controlled them to begin with. All I am responsible for are the things within my power: my beliefs, my thoughts, my emotions, and my actions. Trusting that God has always had my best interests in mind, I respond to life as best I can, according to my understanding of how He would have me respond.

Through acceptance, I have ceased fighting everyone and everything. I see that God is working in others' lives just as He works in mine. Their circumstances are shaped by their choices and by His will for them. Like me, they are works in progress—lost at sea, doing the best they can to find their way home.

I have come to see that much of what lies outside human agency— or our beliefs, thoughts, emotions, and actions—belongs to God in ways I do not fully understand. When I judge others, I risk judging His plan for them based on my limited perspective. When I judge the world and its suffering, I risk assuming I can see more clearly than I truly can.

Acceptance teaches me trust—not because I suddenly understand God's ways, but because I no longer need to. By focusing on what I do have the power to influence—refining my beliefs, nurturing my emotions, disciplining my thoughts, and acting as faithfully as I know how—I leave the outcomes in His hands. At times this brings harmony and peace; at other times it simply allows me to endure what I cannot yet make sense of, trusting that His presence remains.

And if He determines that non self-imposed suffering or adversity is needed—whether through cancer, the death of a loved one, or an atrocity committed against me by another human being—I trust that He is preparing me for eternity in ways I do not fully understand. I trust that He strengthens my spirit, deepening my relationship with Him, growing my faith, and equipping me either to walk through hardship with grace or to overcome it as a witness to His power, mercy, and love.

Remember Jesus in the Garden, bleeding for our sins, suffering in unfathomable ways.

Matthew 26:39
"And He went a little farther, and fell on his face, and prayed, saying, O my Father, if it be possible, let this cup pass from me: nevertheless not as I will, but as thou wilt."

Remember Jesus being scourged, and tortured and having to carry His own cross and then being crucified on it.

Luke 23:46
"And when Jesus had cried with a loud voice, He said, Father,

into Thy hands I commend my Spirit: and having said thus, He gave up the ghost."

God allowed His only Begotten Son to suffer so that His plan of Salvation might be fulfilled. And Jesus humbly and meekly did His part.

Temporal and temporary suffering is just that, temporary. As much as God wants us to find joy in this lifetime, He is more worried about our Eternal salvation.

I trust that He knows what preparation my individual soul requires during this mortal existence. What happens to me and to my physical body is one thing; the Eternal condition of my soul is another. I do not presume to know why such harsh means are sometimes permitted—only that this mortal life is but a twinkling of the eye when set against eternity.

Because of this, I have hope. No matter what unfolds here on earth, if I endure and place my faith in Christ, His grace will be sufficient for me, and I will dwell with Him in peace, love, and harmony forever. He does indeed work in mysterious ways.

Accepting that nothing—absolutely nothing—happens in God's universe by accident frees me from the need to have all the answers. It releases my need to control what I cannot control. It allows me to rest in the knowledge that all of this has meaning, purpose, and direction.

Isaiah 45:7
"I form the light, and create darkness:
I make peace, and create evil:
I the Lord do all these things."

Acceptance gives me the freedom to surrender my life, my will, my desires, and my motives to Him. I do so willingly, because

I no longer see God as a punishing force, but as a loving Father who seeks only to guide His children home—to the serenity of His presence, His love, and His grace.

And I pray:

"Lord, I ask that You might allow me now to accept all that has been, is, and all that will be, that I might continue to understand that Your perfect will, plan, and timing are at work in all things, that although I do not understand Your wisdom, I might accept that it is true and loving, that it is all part of the plan to bring me home again to Thee.

I ask Thee to allow me the courage to not need to understand any of it, the courage to set aside my fearful need to know what it all means.

Lord, I place my trust in Your understanding and wisdom. I humbly and meekly ask You, if it be Thy will, that You might remove my need to know all the answers, that I might enjoy the peace and serenity that placing my trust in Thee provides. Lord please, allow me to lay this burden down.

I love You, Lord. Thank You for always taking care of me and always being there for me.

Amen."

Chapter 6 - Surrender

SURRENDER - Releasing control to God

"Dearest Heavenly Father,
We come to You today humbly and meekly, deeply grateful for all the blessings You have given us. We are grateful for every moment of our lives—both good and bad—because we trust that all of them have been leading us home to You.

We ask You, Lord, if it is Your will, to grant us the wisdom and courage to offer our wills to You—that You might do with them as Thou wilt—that You might shape us and build us into what we need to become in order to live happily in this life and be made whole again with You in eternity.

We have strayed. We have made mistakes. We have taken wrong turns. We have often been deceived—yet You never stopped loving us, Lord. You never stopped loving us.

If it is Your will, we ask that You open our eyes and our ears, and soften our hearts, that we might know You, understand You, and love You more fully.
Your will—not ours—be done. Amen"

When I became willing to do whatever it would take to no longer be that man, or live that life anymore—and when I chose to accept life on life's terms, allowing myself to see His loving hand in all of creation—I laid down some of the heaviest burdens a human being can carry.

I laid down a lifetime of resentment and ignorance.
I laid down the need to control every circumstance of my life.
I laid down the fear that I was not good enough and would

someday pay the price for that insufficiency.
I laid down my pain.
I laid down my suffering.
I laid down my need to control the outcomes and results of my actions.
I laid down my impatience and my need to know all the answers or how everything would end.
I laid down my weaknesses and imperfections.
I laid down my need to be perfect.

Romans 12:1–2 (KJV)

"I beseech you therefore, brethren, by the mercies of God, that ye present your bodies a living sacrifice, holy, acceptable unto God, which is your reasonable service.
And be not conformed to this world: but be ye transformed by the renewing of your mind, that ye may prove what is that good, and acceptable, and perfect, will of God."

Willingness opened my mind and heart. Acceptance allowed me to make peace with my past, my present, and my future. Together, they led me to a place where I became willing—of my own free will and agency—to surrender my will and my life to Him.

I surrendered my dreams, my goals, and my motives, that I might learn to align my life with the plan He has set forth for me. I became willing to accept His plan and surrendered to it. That surrender brought me into harmony with the world—like a leaf that finally stops fighting the wind and releases its grip from the branch. I, like a leaf on the wind, allowed myself to be moved according to His will and His plan, trusting that I would blossom where I was planted.

It was difficult for me to surrender my will to Him. I had taken great pride in my accomplishments, the obstacles I had overcome, and the dark nights I had endured. But looking back—and acknowledging His involvement and power in all of them—loosened the grip that pride had on my heart and mind.

I feared that surrendering my will would cause me to lose myself or diminish my value. I feared that my dreams, goals, and aspirations would be discarded. I feared that relinquishing my imagined control would result in a life I would not want to live—one with less joy, less meaning, and less happiness.

Psalm 37:4–5 (KJV)

"Delight thyself also in the LORD; and He shall give thee the desires of thine heart.
Commit thy way unto the LORD; trust also in Him; and He shall bring it to pass."

Looking back, I can now see how often my own will failed me.

My will sought pleasure, comfort, and provision from imperfect and impermanent sources.
My will relied on imperfect people.
My will relied on possessions that could be lost, stolen, or broken.
My will relied on social standing and financial security, placing me in competition with my brothers and sisters who were also striving for their own security.
My will operated from scarcity—believing there was not enough for everyone, and that I must take more than I needed and withhold it from others.

By seeking peace and contentment from the material world, my will brought me pain, suffering, unrest, fear, and an emptiness in my heart.

Matthew 6:19–21 (KJV)

"Lay not up for yourselves treasures upon earth, where moth and rust doth corrupt, and where thieves break through and steal:
But lay up for yourselves treasures in heaven, where neither moth nor rust doth corrupt, and where thieves do not break through nor steal:
For where your treasure is, there will your heart be also."

What I found in surrender was a peace unlike anything I had ever known—born from humble supplication to a loving Father and from the wisdom to stop seeking peace outside myself, and instead to begin seeking the peace and serenity that had always been available within me.

By no longer needing to control outcomes or understand every detail, my energy was freed to focus on what was actually within my power: my beliefs, my thoughts, my emotions, and my actions.

Surrendering my will to God began a process of purification. As I turned my gaze inward rather than outward, I began to see clearly the things within me that had been the primary sources of my pain, suffering, and failure.

I became aware of my beliefs—both helpful and harmful—and began changing the filters through which I perceived life.
I became aware of my thoughts, learning to pause between stimulus and response.
I became aware of my emotions, recognizing what triggered

them and discerning whether they still served me.
I became aware of my actions, aligning them with my righteous ideal—an ideal rooted in God—and with His will and His plan.

When I surrender my will to God and His plan, I surrender the outcomes to Him. I trust that because He loves me, knows me, and understands my heart, my desires, and my fears, He will provide everything I need to do His will.

When I choose surrender, I stop fighting God and resisting His work in my life.

Matthew 6:25–30 (KJV)

"Therefore I say unto you, Take no thought for your life, what ye shall eat, or what ye shall drink; nor yet for your body, what ye shall put on. Is not the life more than meat, and the body than raiment?

Behold the fowls of the air: for they sow not, neither do they reap, nor gather into barns; yet your heavenly Father feedeth them. Are ye not much better than they?
Which of you by taking thought can add one cubit unto his stature?
And why take ye thought for raiment? Consider the lilies of the field, how they grow; they toil not, neither do they spin:
And yet I say unto you, That even Solomon in all his glory was not arrayed like one of these.
Wherefore, if God so clothe the grass of the field, which today is, and tomorrow is cast into the oven, shall He not much more clothe you, O ye of little faith?"

So how do we go about surrendering our will to God? How do we willingly offer ourselves to Him so that we might be brought back into harmony with God's creation?

Surrender was not a one-time event for me. It began with willingness and acceptance, but it became a daily practice—often hour by hour, moment by moment. Self-will is a habit strengthened by a lifetime of use. I must continually practice surrender and alignment with His will.

Luke 9:23 (KJV)

"If any man will come after me, let him deny himself, and take up his cross daily, and follow me."

I trust that when I take a step toward Him, He takes a step toward me. In accordance with His will, His plan, and His timing.

A few prayers that have helped me—both in the morning and whenever pride, ego, or self-will begins to take control—are these:

"God, I give myself to You.
Shape me and build within me according to Your will.
Remove what stands between me and You.
Take my struggles and use them for good,
that my life may bear witness to Your love, Your peace, and Your plan.
May I walk in Your will always.
Amen."

Or even simpler:

"God, I give You all that I am—good and broken.
Remove what stands in the way of loving You

and loving my brothers and sisters.
May I do Your will always.
Amen."

And simplest of all—usable in any moment, before any decision or action:

"God, Your will—not mine—be done. Amen."

I say these prayers with humility and with a sincere desire to love God as He loves me, and to love others as He loves them. This motive—aligned with Jesus's two great commandments—adds sincerity and power to prayer. I do not surrender for personal gain. I surrender because I love God and humanity. Humility casts aside pride. Unconditional love is a key to power in prayer.

Mark 12:29–31 (KJV)

"And Jesus answered him, The first of all the commandments is, Hear, O Israel; The Lord our God is one Lord:
And thou shalt love the Lord thy God with all thy heart, and with all thy soul, and with all thy mind, and with all thy strength: this is the first commandment.
And the second is like, namely this, thou shalt love thy neighbour as thyself. There is none other commandment greater than these."

Through surrender, I have found a serenity beyond anything I once imagined possible. I have found rest in humility and meekness. I have learned compassion, love, and empathy. I have gained access to a power greater than myself—one that has strengthened and fortified me through the most difficult times of my life.

Through surrender, I have experienced more serenity than I ever could have hoped for. I find a beautiful rest that comes from the humility and meekness it strengthens. I have come to understand what compassion, love, and empathy truly are. It has allowed me to love without condition, a gift beyond measure, a taste of eternity that I can enjoy in the here and now. I have begun to develop a faith in God's plan for me—a faith that allows me to not need to know all the answers or control all the outcomes. A faith that fills my days with hope: hope that Jesus's Atonement has created a path that will lead me home.

A path toward peace.
A path toward Eternal love with Him.

And I pray:

"God, I love You. I trust You.
I have these dreams, and these desires, and these goals for my life that I don't know what to do with.

I don't want to ask any more of You Lord, for You've given me everything I could ever need. You've loved me beyond anything I could ever ask for.

Lord, what do I do with my things? How do I know if they align with Your will? Where does my will end and where does yours begin?

I ask Thee Lord, humbly and meekly, that You might have my dreams, desires, and goals and do with them as You please.

I ask Thee Lord that You might teach me how to pray rightly, and how to know when I'm caught up in my will, that I might adjust my sails properly, that I might do Thy will always. Oh Lord, I bow down before Thee, not because I must, but because I love You so very much.

I know You're here. I feel You, Lord and I trust You with all that I am.

I place myself unreservedly in Thy hands.

You can have my desire, You can have my goals, and You can have my dreams.

I don't want them if I can't have Thee.

Amen."

Part Three:
Trusting God

Chapter 7 - Faith

FAITH — Trusting God Regardless of Proof

The faith we are speaking of is not verified by outcomes or evidence in this world, but grounded in what God has accomplished Eternally through Christ.

The flow of Part Two into Part Three was intentional. Willingness, Acceptance, and Surrender are not faith themselves, but they prepare the ground in which faith can grow. They are the means by which we relinquish control, lay down resistance, and create space in our hearts for faith to breathe, be nurtured, and grow strong.

We can begin by becoming willing—willing to examine our attitudes and beliefs, and willing to allow God into our hearts and to put our trust in Him.

This willingness requires humility: a setting aside of pride and self-reliance, and an honest recognition that we are not God.

We can begin to accept that God is God, God's will is God's will, and God's plan is God's plan—that life happened according to His will and plan, and that there is nothing we can do to change that.

All we can do is change ourselves, oftentimes only with His help.

We can stop resisting reality and begin focusing our energy on strengthening our relationship with God and thus strengthening our faith in Him.

We can choose to surrender our will to His will, aligning ourselves with His greater harmony, providing a peaceful and serene internal environment that will create the space that faith needs to unfold.

By setting aside our reliance on our finite selves and limited power and beginning to rely on His Eternal and infinite power, surrender adds power to faith.

Faith grows when burdens are laid down and we cease from our own works, entering into rest in God. In that rest, we do not change God's will; rather, God's will begins to change us.

As we lay down our reliance on temporal things and temporal proof, our need to find understanding and meaning in temporal things decreases, allowing us to open our minds and hearts to those things which are Eternal. We learn to trust what has always been true: that God created us and is within us, that His grace is sufficient, and that He is faithful to bring us home.

Earlier in this book, we spoke of a time when humanity was whole, and of the fracture that occurred in Eden when Adam and Eve sinned. That fracture created a God sized void in our hearts and set us on a lifelong journey toward healing and reunion with God—toward becoming at one with Him again.

I have found the metaphor of a God-sized void helpful. Within our hearts exists a longing that cannot be satisfied by anything in the temporal world. Yet we spend our lives attempting to fill that void with relationships, personal success, financial security, physical health, power, prestige, and the endless pursuit of people, places, and things.

No matter how hard we try, no matter how sincere our intentions, no matter how well we perform, an Eternal fracture cannot be repaired with temporal means. A God-sized void cannot be filled by anything other than God. It simply does not work.

What this book seeks to help you recognize is the deeply human tendency to search in the world for a solution to a problem that can only be healed one way. Communion with God is restored through faith in Christ's atoning work and sustained by the grace of God—not by human effort. We cannot earn our way back into heaven.

Romans 3:22–26 (KJV)

"Even the righteousness of God which is by faith of Jesus Christ unto all and upon all them that believe: for there is no difference:
For all have sinned, and come short of the glory of God;
Being justified freely by his grace through the redemption that is in Christ Jesus:
Whom God hath set forth to be a propitiation through faith in his blood, to declare his righteousness for the remission of sins that are past, through the forbearance of God;
To declare, I say, at this time his righteousness: that he might be just, and the justifier of him which believeth in Jesus."

Faith is not manufactured by temporal effort. It is received through humility and communion with God. Pride is the great opposition to faith, because pride insists on control, answers, self-sufficiency, and mastery. Faith begins where pride ends.

Faith does not grow through control. It grows in the space created when control ceases.

The scriptures speak repeatedly of God's indwelling presence—not as something we possess by nature, but as something given, sustained, and remembered in grace. When we lay down our burdens and cease striving, we stop looking outside ourselves for what can only be received from God. We turn inward, not to find ourselves, but to encounter the presence of God already at work within us.

As you read the following scriptures, allow them to speak without forcing interpretation. Allow the spirit within you to discern what it means for you.

They repeat this truth again and again—that God is near, that God is within, and that faith is received rather than proven.

Luke 17:21 (KJV)

"Neither shall they say, Lo here! or, lo there! for, behold, the kingdom of God is within you."

John 14:17 (KJV)

"Even the Spirit of truth; whom the world cannot receive, because it seeth Him not, neither knoweth Him: but ye know Him; for He dwelleth with you, and shall be in you."

2 Corinthians 4:6 (KJV)

"For God, who commanded the light to shine out of darkness, hath shined in our hearts, to give the light of the knowledge of the glory of God in the face of Jesus Christ."

John 14:20 (KJV)

"At that day Ye shall know that I am in my Father, and ye in me, and I in You."

Romans 8:10–11 (KJV)

"And if Christ be in you, the body is dead because of sin; but the spirit is life because of righteousness.

But if the Spirit of Him that raised up Jesus from the dead dwell in you, He that raised up Christ from the dead shall also quicken your mortal bodies by His Spirit that dwelleth in you."

1 Corinthians 3:16 (KJV)

"Know ye not that ye are the temple of God, and that the Spirit of God dwelleth in you?"

1 Corinthians 6:19 (KJV)

"What? know ye not that your body is the temple of the Holy Ghost which is in you, which ye have of God, and ye are not your own?"

Ephesians 3:16–17 (KJV)

"That He would grant you, according to the riches of his glory, to be strengthened with might by His Spirit in the inner man; That Christ may dwell in your hearts by faith; that ye, being rooted and grounded in love,"

Colossians 1:27 (KJV)

"To whom God would make known what is the riches of the glory of this mystery among the Gentiles; which is Christ in you, the hope of glory:"

1 John 4:12–13 (KJV)

"No man hath seen God at any time. If we love one another, God dwelleth in us, and his love is perfected in us. Hereby know we that we dwell in Him, and He in us, because He hath given us of His Spirit."

Faith, as I have come to understand it, resists precise definition. It's ambiguous and ethereal. Like grace, it is known more by remembrance than explanation. Words can point toward it, but they cannot define it.

At its deepest level, faith is not the belief that God exists somewhere beyond us, nor confidence that things will turn out as we hope. It is the quiet knowing of relationship — the recognition that God is present, near, and with us. Not "out there," but "in here".

There are moments when faith is no longer something we try to possess or exercise. It becomes trust itself — a resting of the whole self into God. In that place, prayer simplifies. It is no longer asking for outcomes or understanding, but the honest expression of love and surrender: I know You are here. I trust You with all of me.

This is not a trust born of certainty or control, but of love. A trust that says, even without proof and even unto death, You are enough.

Do not trust the world; trust in God. Do not seek proof of eternity in mortality; seek and uncover faith in our hearts—the Kingdom of Heaven which is within us, the presence of a loving Heavenly Father with us.

Proverbs 3:5–6 (KJV)

"Trust in the LORD with all thine heart; and lean not unto thine own understanding.
In all thy ways acknowledge Him, and He shall direct thy paths".

And I pray:

“Lord, I am so very grateful for all the direction and inspiration You have given me, You have never led me astray, and when I wandered You always guided me back.

Lord, I receive great strength in knowing that You are there, that You have a plan for me, that You will never forsake me, that You’ll always be there.

Lord, I’m grateful for all the moments of my life, especially the dark times of my life when I didn’t have enough strength to go on, when I didn’t know how I would ever get through it, when all hope was lost and I stood at the brink of oblivion. I thank You Lord for all my trials of faith that You have provided for me.

Lord, I thank You for always being there for me and for never forsaking me.

I humbly and meekly offer You any remaining doubts or fears that I am holding onto.

Lord, please if it be Thy will, please take them from me. Your will, not mine, be done.

I know Lord that You love me, I know it with all that I am.

I love You so very much Lord.

Amen.”

Chapter 8 - Hope

Hope: Finding Joy in His Timing

Willingness, Acceptance, Surrender, and Faith bring us to a place where we begin to align ourselves toward these truths:

We are not God.

God is God.

God has a plan of salvation.

Christ atoned for our sins to make salvation possible.

God loves us and is with us.

The Spirit of God resides in our hearts and is found when pride is replaced with humility.

The previous four chapters have reshaped the way we relate to God and the way we see both our past and our present. They have cleared the way for us to begin nurturing a living, loving relationship with our Creator, here and now. They have helped us uncover and embrace the gift of Faith that was always present, indwelling, though long obscured—a faith that allows us to face the future with confidence and hope.

How do we now, armed with this renewed understanding of God and our relationship with Him, step forward into the future while remaining aligned with His will and His plan? The answer is hope.

To understand hope rightly and learn how to live it out, we must first look at how hope is expressed in the Old Testament and then how it is transformed in the New Testament—not because hope itself changes, but because the object of hope does.

In the Old Testament, hope in God is most often directed toward temporal realities. It centers on deliverance from enemies, relief from famine, healing from disease, protection from physical harm, material provision, and preservation of life.

Psalm 33:18–19
"Behold, the eye of the LORD is upon them that fear Him, upon them that hope in his mercy;
To deliver their soul from death, and to keep them alive in famine."

Old Testament hope frequently rests on God intervening in the circumstances of life, often accompanied by the expectation that obedience to the Law would influence whether that intervention occurred—hope understood, at times, as a transaction: I have been faithful; God will deliver me.

Psalm 71:4–5
"Deliver me, O my God, out of the hand of the wicked, out of the hand of the unrighteous and cruel man.
For Thou art my hope, O Lord GOD: Thou art my trust from my youth."

Yet scripture is honest in showing that deliverance was not always tied to obedience in a predictable way. At times, the righteous suffered while the wicked prospered. Obedience to the Law did not guarantee favorable outcomes.

Ecclesiastes 9:2
"All things come alike to all: there is one event to the righteous, and to the wicked; to the good and to the clean,

and to the unclean; to him that sacrificeth, and to him that sacrificeth not: as is the good, so is the sinner; and he that sweareth, as he that feareth an oath."

Hope grounded solely in temporal resolution is fragile. When hope depends on circumstances improving—circumstances always subject to God's will—it is never guaranteed. In an imperfect and impermanent world, the only certainty of which is death.

This is a hope that quietly says, "I will love You and trust You as long as life unfolds the way I expect." It is love and trust with conditions.

In the New Testament, hope is given an Eternal objective. Through the Atonement of Jesus Christ, hope is transformed and energized by faith, no longer anchored to outcomes in time but to promises beyond it. Hope, joined with faith and love, rests on Eternal realities—perfect in nature—and therefore produces enduring results.

Hebrews 7:19
"For the law made nothing perfect, but the bringing in of a better hope did; by the which we draw nigh unto God."

Hope in eternal life made possible through the Atonement of Christ and the grace of God—reshapes our entire perspective. It changes the meaning of mortality itself and transforms how we respond to suffering, loss, and trial.

Romans 5:1–4
"Therefore being justified by faith, we have peace with God through our Lord Jesus Christ:
By whom also we have access by faith into this grace wherein we stand, and rejoice in hope of the glory of God."

And not only so, but we glory in tribulations also: knowing that tribulation worketh patience;
And patience, experience; and experience, hope:

Through hope, joined with faith and love, we are able to weather the storms of life with joy in our hearts. We come to see that a lifetime of suffering is a small price to pay for an eternity of peace, love, and grace with God.

This is a hope that says, "I will love and trust You no matter what happens here on Earth."

This hope produces steadfastness of spirit and patient endurance in all things related to our mortal existence. It allows us to rest in the knowledge that God's timing is perfect and that His purposes will ultimately lead us back to Him.

This hope turns struggle into peace, longing into contentment, doubt into knowing, impatience into serenity. It transforms separation into reunion, pain into growth, suffering into understanding, fear into courage, and despair into comfort.

This hope in His perfect plan enables us to endure the full range of life's vicissitudes. It becomes His comforting hand, lifting us and carrying us when life overwhelms us and we feel unable to continue. And as we endure in grace, this hope bears witness to others—quietly reflecting His peace and His perfect love.

Matthew 5:16
"Let your light so shine before men, that they may see your good works, and glorify your Father which is in heaven."

And I pray:

"Lord, I come to You today grateful for all the love that You have given me.

I thank You for allowing Your Son Jesus Christ to walk amongst us, to love us, to teach us, and for all that He sacrificed for us.

I am grateful today for Christ's Atonement and the path that it has revealed to us, a path that leads us home to Thee.

Lord, my heart longs for Thy presence and delights knowing that one day we will be together again.

I ask Thee Lord, if it be Thy will, that You allow the light of hope to always shine within my heart and mind, that it might shine upon those who are walking through dark times in their lives, that I might become an instrument of Your love, peace, and grace upon this earth.

Lord, I love Thee so.

I patiently await our reunion, humbly, meekly, and gratefully.

Amen."

Chapter 9 - Love

LOVE — At One in Christ

1 Corinthians 13:13 (KJV)
"And now abideth faith, hope, charity, these three; but the greatest of these is charity."

The love scripture calls us to is not sentiment or affection, but what Paul names charity — agapē — self-giving, enduring, Eternal Love.

This is the love we will be focusing on in this chapter. Love that, when joined with faith and hope, makes the path before us clear. The love that brings alignment, direction, and certainty to the journey of the soul. The love that draws us toward reunion with Him in eternity.

Matthew 7:13–14 (KJV)
"Enter ye in at the strait gate: for wide is the gate, and broad is the way, that leadeth to destruction, and many there be which go in thereat:
Because strait is the gate, and narrow is the way, which leadeth unto life, and few there be that find it."

This path was laid forth since the beginning of time — narrow and straight — leading not to destruction, but to life. Faith gives us the power to step onto it. Hope gives us the strength to endure it. Love gives us the light by which we walk it. Together, faith, hope, and Love become a torch, illuminating the way and leading us home to Him.

Matthew 5:48 (KJV)
"Be ye therefore perfect (complete or whole), even as your
Father which is in heaven is perfect (complete or whole)."

Because the nature of God is Complete and Whole, therefore the nature of love, which is of God, is also Complete and Whole. Jesus tells us to love Him with all that we are, with all of our heart, all of our soul, all of our mind, because that's how He loves us.

He loves us without agenda, without conditions, without expectation, without the need for reciprocation, without borders, boundaries, or degrees, without exclusion, without reservation, wholly, flawlessly, completely, totally, now and forever.

Love is a remembrance of when we were once one with Him and each other in eternity. It's a remembrance of how we will be again one with Him and each other in eternity.

John 17:24 (KJV)
"Father, I will that they also, whom Thou hast given me, be
with me where I am; that they may behold my glory, which
Thou hast given me: for Thou lovedst me before the
foundation of the world."

Love is a witness to this, and bears testimony of this.

Romans 8:38–39 (KJV)
"For I am persuaded, that neither death, nor life, nor angels,
nor principalities, nor powers, nor things present, nor things
to come,
Nor height, nor depth, nor any other creature, shall be able to
separate us from the Love of God, which is in Christ Jesus
our Lord."

Love is a shared remembrance of our oneness with each other. It is a recognition of the Eternal nature in each of us, we being children of God, loved perfectly by a loving Father in Heaven.

Love remembers a time when we lived with one another in perfect peace and harmony, before pride separated us from each other and from God. Love rejoices, knowing that we will all be reunited together again.

John 17:21–23 (KJV)
"That they all may be one; as Thou, Father, art in me, and I in Thee, that they also may be one in us: that the world may believe that Thou hast sent me.
And the glory which Thou gavest me I have given them; that they may be one, even as we are one:
I in them, and Thou in me, that they may be made perfect in one; and that the world may know that Thou hast sent me, and hast loved them, as Thou hast loved me."

Jesus, with His two Great Commandments, is really showing us the way home through Love, away from separation born from sin, and toward a loving communion with God. Love guides us and directs us, like a compass, toward a truth long forgotten.

Matthew 22:37–39 (KJV)
"Jesus said unto him, Thou shalt Love the Lord thy God with all thy heart, and with all thy soul, and with all thy mind.
This is the first and great commandment.
And the second is like unto it, Thou shalt Love thy neighbour as thyself."

Love remembers and longs for a union that our mind and hearts have forgotten. Our mind and heart, creations of a mortal existence, are limited and shrouded by the veil between eternity and mortality. Love hints at a time forgotten, and hints at the glory to come when we are reunited with Him in eternity.

We must soften our hearts and turn them toward Him;

2 Corinthians 3:14–16 (KJV)
"But their minds were blinded: for until this day remaineth the same veil untaken away in the reading of the old testament; which veil is done away in Christ.
But even unto this day, when Moses is read, the veil is upon their heart.
Nevertheless when it shall turn to the Lord, the veil shall be taken away."

Where sin and mortality shroud and hide us from the truth, Love uncovers and shines His light, showing us our true identity as Children of a loving God.

Where sin brings separation, Love brings reunion.
Where sin brings fear, Love brings faith.
Where sin brings despair, Love brings hope.
Where sin brings regret, Love brings forgiveness.
Where sin brings struggle, Love brings rest.
Where sin brings sorrow, Love brings joy.
Where sin brings discord, Love brings peace and harmony.
Where sin leads to death and darkness, Love lights the way to eternal life.

The burdens we carry — pride, self-reliance, selfishness, resentment, hopelessness, anger, unresolved grief, shame, perfectionism, lust — strengthen that separation and prevent us from loving Him as He loves us and from loving our neighbors as He loves them. That's why it's critical that we begin laying our burdens down, removing those things within us that separate us from our loving Father and separate us from one another.

1 John 4:10–12 (KJV)
"Herein is love, not that we loved God, but that He loved us, and sent his Son to be the propitiation for our sins.
Beloved, if God so loved us, we ought also to love one another.
No man hath seen God at any time. If we love one another, God dwelleth in us, and his love is perfected in us."

Love, as witnessed and experienced through the Atonement of Christ — Christ loving us so much that He bled for our sins, allowed himself to be tortured and crucified, so that we might be able to find our way back to our Heavenly Father, where we can live with Him and each other in perfect love for eternity.

Your Heavenly Father loves you. Let your faith in His Love strengthen you and give you hope that you might endure to the end, that you might be reunited with Him in eternity. Amen.

John 3:16–17 (KJV)
"For God so loved the world, that He gave his only begotten Son, that whosoever believeth in Him should not perish, but have everlasting life.
For God sent not his Son into the world to condemn the world; but that the world through Him might be saved."

And I pray:

"Lord, my loving Heavenly Father, I humbly and meekly come before you, a loving child, grateful for Your warmth, provision, and guidance as I find my way home to Thee.

I'm grateful today for the love in my heart for Thee and for my brothers and sisters, Your beloved children, one and all.

I ask Thee Lord, if it be Thy will, that You might allow me to continue to lay those things down within me that prevent me from loving You and loving them as Your Son Jesus Christ did, that I might ever grow in His image and likeness, that in me You might be well pleased.

Lord, I ask Thee with all that I am, that You might allow us to love one another, that we might set aside those things that separate us, that we might be one and whole again in Christ,

Amen."

Part Four:
Resting in Grace

Chapter 10 - A Loving Moral Inventory

Uncover and Discover Our Burdens So We Can Then Lay Them Down

In this chapter we will look inward—honestly, lovingly, and rigorously—identify the burdens in our lives that are wearing us down and preventing us from loving ourselves, loving our neighbors, and loving God.

We will approach this in two parts:

Discovery

Understanding

This chapter is not about beating yourself up or self-condemnation. It's not about shame, blame, or regret. It's about healing ourselves mentally, emotionally, and spiritually so that we might love more fully and unconditionally, feel more joy, strengthen our faith, increase the hope in our lives, and bring our will and our lives into closer harmony with His will and His plan for us and for creation.

This process is very simple—not easy, but simple. This may be one of the most difficult things you ever do in your life, but just to the degree that it is difficult, you will experience that degree of relief. The more thorough you are, the more burdens you will be able to lay down. The deeper the wounds and burdens you discover, the deeper the transformation.

This is your inventory. Regardless of how thorough this initial pass is, or how deep you go, learning this process will develop a skill you can return to whenever you are ready—or whenever the Spirit prompts you to increase your awareness.

At times you may say, "I'm not ready to lay down that burden yet. It's still a big part of who I am and what I believe, and I just don't think I can do it."

This inventory isn't about becoming perfect now, or even in this lifetime. It's about awareness and shining light on those things that have been kept in darkness.

Your life will tell you when you're ready to lay your burdens down. It will compel you to do so in accordance with His plan and His will for you. It will give you the willingness necessary when you are ready to allow Him to take these things from you.

There is no pressure, no timetable, and no expectation. There is no right or wrong way to do this.
You are safe here, and you are not being judged.
This is an act of love—a cooperative effort with God.
Your Heavenly Father loves you. Everything is already okay.

The first time I did this inventory, I came up with 49 burdens that were separating me from God and preventing me from loving people as He loves people. Things like insecurities in relationships and how they manifested themselves to the detriment of all involved. Things like being dishonest to mask my low self-esteem and fear of failure. There was the regret and shame I carried for all the times I treated my mother and father poorly and the things I put them through. There was the regret, shame, and pain I held about the times I acted in a less-than-loving way toward my children and my wife.

There were the resentments I carried and the beliefs I had adopted from those who hurt me physically in my life. There were the laws I had broken that resulted from my desire to fit in and be accepted. There was my judgment of others and my gossiping about others, all stemming from not feeling like I was good enough. There were all of my addictions that controlled much of my life—alcohol, drugs, food, pornography. There were all of my character defects and personality flaws that made living life among other human beings more difficult than it needed to be—defects that prevented me from forming meaningful, healthy, and lasting relationships with others and from loving others without condition or expectation.

There were all of my sins, staring me right in the face—exposing my pride, lust, envy, gluttony, wrath, and greed— and leaving me nowhere to hide. This inventory was like a mirror, revealing myself to me, showing me the error of my ways, showing me where pride and self-reliance had failed me. The act of getting all of this out of me, putting it on paper, and seeking to gain a better understanding of its true causes was an absolutely life-changing event for me.

Since doing my first inventory, I have completed two more full inventories and more spot-check inventories than I could possibly remember. Having done this, as the first step in the process of laying down my burdens, I became willing to allow Him to enter my heart, heal me, and love me. I let Him into my heart to an extent that I never had before.

I share these very personal things with you because I sincerely want you to get the most out of this inventory that you can. I share them because this was the most important thing I have ever done to grow as a person and to remove those things that had separated me from God. I share them because, even though we have never met, I can honestly say that I love you—and the only reason I can honestly say that is because I did this inventory. I share them so you can see how deep this can go and to give you the courage to dig as deep as you can.

Preparing the Inventory

Go ahead and take out a piece of paper—preferably a notebook, as you will need more than one page, and there is value in keeping it all together in one place. This work will become sacred to you, and being able to look back on it in the future and see where you were and how far you have come will become an invaluable blessing and a gift.

A couple of inches from the left side of the page draw a line from top to bottom, creating two columns, the one on the left narrow, the one on the right the rest of the page. In column one you will write down your burdens. In column two you will understand the nature of each burden. When you enter a burden in the left column, leave five or so lines between each one, as you will be doing some writing in the right column. Optimally, you should have four to five burdens per sheet of paper.

You will run through the lists provided—common manifestations of burdens—to identify those things that separate you from love, peace, joy, and God. We are not looking for a total or perfect list of burdens, although the more thorough you are, the more burdens you will be able to lay down. If you don't acknowledge that a burden is there, you cannot lay it down.

Be honest with yourself. If you feel like you might have a burden but aren't sure, write it down so you can seek the truth of it in the right column. More will be revealed. Think of this as a guided brainstorm. There are no wrong answers and no judgment. God is with you and loves you.

Write everything down that you're carrying and no longer want—all the things within you that are sources of pain, suffering, disharmony, fear, doubt, or anything that is not serving you or God any longer.

Once you have completed this work, we will offer these burdens to God, and with His help, guidance, and love, we will lay them down.

1. Discovery

We will be segmenting our search for burdens into five categories:

Obvious Flaws or Character Defects

Resentments and Regrets

Sex Issues

Harms Endured and Committed

Fears

I know this might seem like a lot, but it will go pretty fast once you decide to commit the time and actually begin putting pen to paper. Once you begin, it will take on a life of its own.

Read this list slowly, pausing on each example and allowing the time and space for truth to be revealed.

If you feel overwhelmed, choose only 5 items total today—one from each category—or even just 3 from any category. Or feel free to just focus on the main ones that jump out at you, circle the rest that resonate with you. You can always return later. The key is to make a beginning of it. Take that first step necessary so that God can step in and guide your path.

If any item brings intense distress; pause, pray, and consider doing this with a trusted person or professional support.

Pray and ask God to open your eyes so that you might see, open your ears so that you might hear, and open your heart so that you might receive His guidance and direction. Ask that He might show you not only the things you already know, but especially those things you are unaware of that separate you from Him and His will and His plan, and those that separate you from your brothers and sisters.

Obvious Flaws or Character Defects

This section is about noticing what disrupts love and peace in your life, not judging yourself for having it.

Write down any flaws or character defects that you know you are struggling with. These will be fairly obvious—there is no need to struggle with this.

Ask yourself, with honesty, humility, and love: Am I carrying any of the following burdens in my life?

Write all that apply in column one.

Pride

Arrogant

Vain

Egotistical

Self-righteous

Morally superior

Judgmental

Defensive

Hypocritical

Dishonest

Embellishing the truth

Perfectionist

Obsessive

Impatient

Intolerant

Harsh

Cruel

Angry

Bitter

Cynical

Pessimistic

Complaining

Victim mentality

Self-pity

Procrastination

Lazy

Self-centered

Need to be right

Need to be admired

Needy

Approval-seeking

People-pleasing

Controlling

Manipulative

Addiction (substances, behaviors, thought patterns)

Self-reliant to the exclusion of God

Resentments and Regrets

This section is about acknowledging where pain has been held—toward others or yourself—so it no longer has to be carried alone.

Resentments

Now ask yourself if you are holding any resentments toward any of the people, groups, or institutions listed below.

Write down all that apply in column one.

Parents

Siblings

Children

Spouse / partner

Former partners

Friends

Former friends

Employers

Managers

Coworkers

Employees

Mentors

Authority figures

Religious leaders

Teachers

Institutions

Organizations

Government

Society

Groups

Strangers

Abusers

Neglectful caregivers

Those who betrayed us

Those who rejected us

Those who misunderstood us

Those who judged us

Those who disappointed us

Ourselves

God

Regrets

Now ask yourself if you are holding any regrets from the examples below.

Write all that apply in column one, with a brief description of who, what, and when.

Things said in anger

Things left unsaid

Relationships damaged or abandoned

Opportunities not taken

Boundaries not set

Boundaries violated

Staying too long

Leaving too soon

Choosing fear over love

Choosing comfort over growth

Choosing pride over humility

Choosing control over trust

Choices made in addiction

Choices made in fear

Choices made to be liked

Parenting regrets

Relationship regrets

Career regrets

Financial regrets

Spiritual neglect

Missed time

Missed presence

Missed love

Sex Issues

This section touches on a very sensitive subject. Allow yourself to be honest with yourself and to keep an open mind and an open heart. There is no judgment here, only recognition.

Write down all that apply in column one, with a brief description of who, what, and when.

Undesirable Sexual Traits / Patterns

Lust

Objectification

Compulsivity

Escapism through sex

Using sex to soothe pain

Using sex for validation

Using sex for control

Using sex for power

Using sex for worth

Emotional detachment

Emotional dependency

Shame-based sexuality

Secret sexual behaviors

Double lives

Fantasy reliance

Pornography use

Compulsive masturbation

Distorted Sexual Beliefs

My worth is tied to desirability

Sex equals love

Sex equals acceptance

Sex equals safety

Sex equals power

Sex equals connection

Sex is owed

Sex is transactional

Sex fixes loneliness

Sex proves masculinity / femininity

Desire is dangerous

Desire is shameful

Desire must be suppressed

Desire must be indulged

Manipulation

Deception

Infidelity

Emotional affairs

Boundary violations

Coercion

Using another for self-gain

Endured

Objectification

Emotional neglect

Sexual neglect

Boundary violations

Coercion

Abuse

Shame imposed

Silence imposed

Harms Endured and Committed

This section is about seeing the truth about harms, without falling into guilt, blame, or self-condemnation.

Now ask yourself if you have ever hurt others or been hurt by others in the following ways.

Write all that apply in column one, with a brief description of who, what, and when.

Neglect

Abandonment

Rejection

Betrayal

Abuse (physical, emotional, sexual, spiritual)

Gaslighting

Humiliation

Control

Violence

Emotional invalidation

Conditional love

Betrayal

Manipulation

Emotional withdrawal

Neglect

Harsh words

Silence as punishment

Control

Using others

Abandonment

Infidelity

Breaking trust

Withholding love

Fears

This section is about recognizing how fear has been an instrument of darkness in our lives. By increasing your understanding of it you allow the light of love, faith and hope to take its place.

Now ask yourself if you have experienced any of the following fears in your lifetime.

Write all that apply in column one, with a brief description of who, what, and when.

Fear of abandonment

Fear of rejection

Fear of being unlovable

Fear of being unseen

Fear of being insignificant

Fear of being powerless

Fear of being wrong

Fear of being exposed

Fear of shame

Fear of failure

Fear of success

Fear of intimacy

Fear of vulnerability

Fear of dependence

Fear of surrender

Fear of losing control

Fear of uncertainty

Fear of suffering

Fear of death

Fear of trusting God

2. Understanding

Before you begin working in column two, reread column one. Ask God to show you any trends, patterns, or inspiration He may provide. Also ask yourself, "Is there anything in me that I am carrying that I did not put down?" Allow yourself the time necessary to see what you need to see, hear what you need to hear, and feel what you need to feel.

Now, one burden at a time, ask yourself the following questions. On each question, pause and allow the time and space needed for the truth to be revealed. Write all insight and answers into column two.

What are all the situations this burden manifested in? Write them all down.

What is the earliest instance I can remember of this burden?

Why do I believe I have it? Where do I believe it came from?

Who have I hurt with this burden? How have I hurt them?

When did I hurt myself with this burden? In what ways did I hurt myself?

What trials and adversity have I created with this burden?

Now—and this is important—take a moment to relax. Focus on what humility means to you. Focus on what meekness means to you. Remember that you are not God; God is God. God is your Father, and God loves you. You are a child of God. Take a moment to feel what that means and all that it implies.

Now look at everything you have written and read it in two ways. First, read one column at a time from top to bottom, again looking for patterns and asking if anything has been left out. Second, read burden by burden, moving from column one to column two, one at a time, line upon line. Allow yourself to be mentally and emotionally full—pouring all that you are and have into this process humbly, meekly, and lovingly.

Let all of this settle. The Spirit of God is now working in you and through you. Allow Him the time and space to do what He needs to do. Give yourself the time and space necessary to regain your strength and prepare for what comes next. Rest—you have done much. Rest—you will need your strength for what is to come.

And I pray:

"Lord, be with me now in my time of need.

I humbly and meekly invite You into my being, that You might comfort me, steady me, and give me the strength necessary to carry these burdens until I am ready and able to lay them down.

I ask Thee Lord, if it be Thy will, that You shine Your Light upon my darkness, that You might embrace my heart with Your perfect Love, that You might guide my thoughts with Your perfect Wisdom, that You might fortify my body with Your perfect Power.

Lord, as it is pride that separated me from Thee, it is with all humility that I kneel before Thee now.

I thank Thee for my trespasses. I thank Thee for my sins. I thank Thee for the trials and tribulations of my life, and all the pain and suffering therein.

Though I walk through the valley of the shadow of death, I do so gratefully knowing that it is Your merciful path away from an eternity bereft of Your love, peace, and grace.

I love You Lord with all that I am. Amen."

Chapter 11 - Lay Them Down

Lay Them Down

Now that we have written down the burdens and sought to understand them and see how they manifest itself in our lives, I'm gonna have you run them through on more filter before we start talking about strategies to begin laying them down. This question is very important, as to lay them down, we need to make sure He is ready for us to do so.

Pull out your work, and with each burden I want you to ask yourself one simple question; Has He in the past, or is He now, using this burden to shape me? God can use our defects as a means of direction, He uses them as a way to help us grow into the person He would have us become, He can use them as an instrument of His will in our lives.

2 Corinthians 12:7–10 (KJV)

"And lest I should be exalted above measure through the abundance of the revelations, there was given to me a thorn in the flesh, the messenger of Satan to buffet me, lest I should be exalted above measure.
For this thing I besought the Lord thrice, that it might depart from me.
And He said unto me, My grace is sufficient for thee: for my strength is made perfect in weakness. Most gladly therefore will I rather glory in my infirmities, that the power of Christ may rest upon me.
Therefore I take pleasure in infirmities, in reproaches, in

necessities, in persecutions, in distresses for Christ's sake: for when I am weak, then am I strong."

God used a thorn of Satan to keep Paul humble lest He be exalted above measure.

Ask yourself these questions as you run down the list of burdens you have set before you. How could God have used this burden to teach me? How does my greater understanding of this burden serve to help God and others? Is there still a lesson in this burden that I need to learn, so that I might finally be able to lay it down? Search your soul, you'll know the truth when you come across it, if at all.

1 Timothy 1:15–16 (KJV)

"This is a faithful saying, and worthy of all acceptation, that Christ Jesus came into the world to save sinners; of whom I am chief.
Howbeit for this cause I obtained mercy, that in me first Jesus Christ might shew forth all longsuffering, for a pattern to them which should hereafter believe on Him to life everlasting."

I feel like when I chose wrong in life, chose my will over His will, that God will continue to present me with opportunities to choose rightly until I learn the lesson He would have me learn. I believe that God give make up tests. Looking at the situations surrounding the sin, character defect, flaw, etc... Is there wisdom, understanding, learning, or guidance to be had?

Looking at our inventories, we have a lot of burdens to consider. Where do we begin and how do we go about finally laying them down, allowing us to find more peace, love, and joy in our lives, now?

This is too much to do all at once, and often it can take quite a long time to finally make peace with all of it. Sometimes it can take a lifetime. I remember, 6 years after my first Loving Moral Inventory, I sat at my desk in the early morning doing a gratitude list. I was suddenly overcome with great joy and gratitude like I had never known. Tears pouring down my face, I said out loud;

"Enough Kyle. It's enough. All of the moments of your life have been forgiven."

All of the moments of my life were already forgiven by God. Most of them had been forgiven by others long before that morning. It took me 6 years though, of diligent and devoted work, to finally get to a point where I could forgive myself for my part in all the moments of my life. I had carried those burdens for so long. To finally be able to lay them down was a blessing and a gift.

So again, we're not looking for perfection, we're just trying to take that first step toward Him.

I would like to break the rest of this Chapter into 3 parts, all of them aimed at helping you to lay your burdens down.

1. Confession and Communion with God

2. Amends

3. Forgiveness

1. Confession and Communion with God

What I am going to ask you to do now is one of the most difficult things I've ever experienced in my life, but is also one of the most rewarding and transformational moments of my life.

What you will do now is read this inventory, one burden at a time, column one naming the burden, column two reading the understanding, to another human being. You are reading this to another human being to humble yourself before God. When we humble ourselves before God, it allows Him access so He might use us and shape us as He will.

It's very important that you find someone you can trust completely to read this to. Someone who will not judge you or try to change you. You will be revealing all that you are to this human being in the sight of God.

You will be flaying your soul open, allowing God full access to change you and remove the burdens that He knows are separating you from Him and preventing you from becoming the person He created you to become.

Think pastors, bishops, clergy men, parents, siblings, best friends, etc. It's very important though that you pick someone who will not be harmed by what you read to them. It's not fair to clear our conscience at the expense of another.

If you absolutely cannot or will not, that is totally ok, as this is your inventory of your burdens and is sacred and should be protected. So, if the human needed is not available to you, you can also read this into a mirror or read it to the ocean or read it to the forest, making sure to pray beforehand that He give you the courage needed to let Him all the way in.

There is no right or wrong way to do this, but there are some things to consider that may help optimize the experience for you. I find when reading this to another human being, they can get uncomfortable and they might feel the need to stop you and console you and love you. This is a beautiful human tendency, to comfort and love, but in this case, it can possibly be a detriment. They may try and stop you, which may be what God intends or not, but it can make it difficult to get through the entire inventory and can take away any spiritual momentum that you have created. I would ask them to please hold their comments and advice until the end, or if they must interject that it might be brief and to the point.

Please plan ahead and allow yourself time to be alone with God when you're done reading. Give yourself an hour or so to rest, surrender, pray, and allow the feelings and thoughts that come up to run their course. Do not fight them. Just witness them. If they give you pain or if fear sets in just offer that pain and that fear to God. He is working in you now. Trust Him. Let Him all the way in. He needs to bring things to the surface so they can be removed. It's all part of the process.

My Personal Witness

This doesn't have to go smoothly or perfectly; it just needs to happen. We have to create space in our souls so God can rush in and fill it.

I read my first inventory to my AA sponsor. I had 49 burdens to read, including the understanding portion of the inventory I had over 12 pages to read. Your inventory doesn't need to be this big, or it can be bigger. All that matters is that you were as honest and thorough as you could be.

While reading this inventory to my sponsor, he kept trying to encourage me and love me, and as kind as that was, it was taking up time. It was so difficult to read these things to another human being, I felt my strength wavering, my resolve slipping, I felt the desire to only read part of it and keep some to myself.

I just wanted to get through it. I didn't want any of this weight any longer, I wanted to lay these burdens down so bad. They were the source of all my suffering and pain and failings my whole life. I had been hurt badly, and I had hurt others, which pained me even more. I didn't want it. I wanted God to please take it all from me. I was broken.

I ended up leaving my sponsor's apartment with the reading unfinished, not because he did anything wrong, but because I was overwhelmed and afraid and just needed to be alone with God. I was afraid and weak and tired, and I ran.

I drove home and prayed to God; I didn't want any of this baggage any longer.

The thought occurred to me, from the Spirit of God, that I needed to finish what I started and call my dad.

I called my dad and he answered. I was tired and crying and told him that I just needed him to listen to me. I didn't need him to understand me or console me; I just needed him to please listen to me to which he agreed.

I continued reading my inventory to my father, line upon line, burden upon burden. When addressing things to him I felt his pain and felt that he wanted to console me, but he allowed me to proceed. He allowed me to pour my soul out to him. What a gift it was to be able to share this with my father. A great blessing indeed.

When I was finally done reading my inventory, I told my dad that I loved him and that I needed to be alone with God. He understood and told me that he loved me.

I then put down the phone and laid down on my living room floor.

I humbly and meekly and gratefully offered myself to God, I offered myself a living sacrifice to Him. I asked Him to please, if it be His will, that He might remove these things from me, that He might take away my pain.

I laid there for a good hour. Resting.

I felt so numb, a numbness born from great effort and the comfort of a loving God. Feelings welled up in me and fell away. Thoughts rose up and fell away. I just watched them and allowed them. I prayed continuously.

Something to the extent of; "Please God, I love You. Please God, help me. Please God, please. I trust You Lord. I know You know what I need and what's best for me. All I want is to love and be loved. Your will, not mine, be done. Your will, not mine, be done. Thank You Lord. Thank You Lord. Thank You…"

As the hour progressed, I noticed something changing inside me. I didn't know what it was, I couldn't tell you where it was inside of me that this was happening, I just felt like I had been changed.

I felt like I'd been living my whole life in a windowless room, and all of a sudden, a wall was removed and the sun poured in. It was uncomfortable — this feeling of a stark contrast between two realities — but it felt safe, and it felt right.

Over the next few days, I noticed that I had indeed been changed somehow. I felt different emotionally and mentally. I felt like some things had been removed from me.

The pain and weight surrounding the moments I had been molested had been removed from me, root and branch. Gone. He took them from me. How glorious is God. He took them from me. My insecurities born from those molestations were noticeably weakened.

I felt the pain and weight surrounding my divorce, my marriage and family broken in part by the hands of my alcoholism, I felt that somehow, I was able to begin to forgive myself for my part in it. It was over. I couldn't change it. All I could do was love my children and show my gratitude and appreciation for everything my wife ever did for me.

I felt my need for the approval of others had decreased, I felt my desire to be rigorously honest with others and myself had increased. There were so many other subtle changes — subtle yet noticeable — in the way I felt and thought. Change had indeed happened.

Other than the pain around my molestation being removed, the other burdens remained. Although a lot of them felt diminished somehow, my grip loosened on them, and I felt like now I could finally take the steps necessary to begin laying them down—one burden at a time, one day at a time. Not perfectly. Not miraculously. But systematically and diligently, as I became ready to release them, in accordance with His will, His plan, His timing. As I mentioned earlier, it took me 6 years to finally forgive myself for my part in all of it.

I forgave myself for not acting lovingly toward my children and wife.

I forgave myself for being dishonest and lying and cheating.

I forgave myself for not telling my grandfather how much he meant to me before he passed.

I forgave myself for failing as a youth, dropping out of the ninth grade, getting hooked on drugs and the shame and regret that accompanied that.

I forgave myself for all the times I hurt my parents, harsh unloving words spoken, the lies I told them, stealing from them.

I forgave myself for all the relationships harmed by my insecurities, my pride, my need to be in control, my manipulation, my fears.

And I believe, most importantly, I forgave myself for turning my back on God. For cursing Him and resenting Him. I knew that He had always been there for me, I always knew it, but I kept Him at arm's length and withdrew my love from Him and it broke my heart like nothing else.

I was always forgiven by Him, but I was finally able to lay that great burden down and find rest for my soul within Him.

It takes what it takes. I promise you though that this will pass. Any pain or regret or shame that you are holding onto will pass away in time, for when this is all over, there is perfect healing and forgiveness in eternity. If we must endure our burden until the end, He will give us the strength and hope to do so if we continue to turn to Him.

We just need to continue to do our part, with His help and guidance, to lay these burdens down and forgive and be forgiven.

2. Amends

We have hurt and injured others in our lives. Whether we meant to hurt them or not, we need to take steps to make it right temporally, so that we might begin to forgive ourselves.

We can't make someone forgive us. We can't make them feel better about the situation. They may never let it go. They may resent us until the end of time. There's nothing we can do about that. That's between them and God and, as such, none of our business.

What is our business is our willingness. We can say we're sorry and mean it. We can humble ourselves and ask for forgiveness. We can be willing to do the things necessary to repay what was stolen or what is owed. We can be willing to fix, however we can, that which was broken. We can be willing to make restitution in any reasonable way that we can to that person or situation.

We never want to make amends where those amends might hurt them or anyone else. This is critical. Who are we to seek to clear our conscience at the expense of the other person? We just can't do it. If we make direct amends to someone, they must be safe, selfless, and in the best interest of that human being. We need to be willing to carry this burden forever, if necessary, rather than hurt someone else again. This is our cross to bear.

Direct amends come in the form of a formal apology, a debt being paid directly to the person owed, or an offer to make things right to the person involved in a way that would seem acceptable to them. We cannot assume what form restitution should be made in. We need to keep an open mind and a willing heart, and be willing to listen to them, as it is us that harmed them. We don't need to accept any unreasonable terms. We don't need to do anything that would harm ourselves. We just need to be willing to listen and love them. That's it.

If we cannot make direct amends to the person because it will harm them or others, or because they are not around or accessible, we can make an indirect amends.

Indirect amends may include writing a letter to them, being as honest as we can about why we did what we did, and expressing our sincere desire to make things right. That letter can be read out loud—to a mirror, at the ocean, or into the forest— and then offer it up to God in prayer, asking that the other person receive that message in a way that can help them find closure and forgiveness in their hearts. Then burn it or destroy it. It's over. You've done what you can do.

We can then do something kind, loving, and selfless for another person, institution, or charity, all in the name of the person we are making the amends to, dedicating that act to the one we have offended.

We can also make living amends. Through a living amends, we show them, ourselves, and God that we are sincerely sorry by choosing not to do whatever we did again. We do this by replacing our sin with its corresponding virtue.

If we were unkind, we can choose to act kindly toward everyone we encounter. If we were unloving, we can choose to love God and humanity with all that we are. If we were dishonest, we can choose to be completely honest, especially if doing so is to our detriment.

If we were greedy, we can choose to freely give of what we have, but more importantly give of what and who we are, to others. If we hurt them lustfully, we can choose to be chaste and pure in our acts and deeds moving forward.

If we hurt them selfishly, judgmentally, or pridefully, we can choose to humble ourselves before God and realize that they too are His children—not below us or above us, but equal to us—that we might accept them exactly as they are in this moment and treat them with the respect, appreciation, and love they deserve.

Some of the most important amends I needed to make were to those I loved the most—those I hurt with my actions and words spoken during my alcoholism.

When I was in the depths of my disease, I remember my wife of 17 years telling me that I needed to quit drinking or she would leave me. Rather than doing the right thing and honoring my marriage and my family, I chose to honor my pride. She left me, and it split our family in two. Now, this wasn't the only reason our marriage failed, but I have to own the fact that my choices had a lot to do with it. I had to completely and wholly own my part in it.

I made amends to my wife by telling her how much I regretted the choices that I made that day. I told her how much I appreciated everything that she ever did for me: for teaching me how to live life as an adult, for supporting me all those years, for giving me the gift of two beautiful children. I told her that she was an answer to my prayers and that I wouldn't be anywhere without her. I told her that I loved her and always would.

I made amends to my children, telling them how sorry I was for the things that I had done and the things that I had said that hurt them. For years to come, I humbled myself before them and allowed myself to hear them when they reminded me of how I acted, and to be with them as they worked through it all and found it in their hearts to forgive me. I still think to this day they might hold onto some things they may or may not be aware of. I know how our relationships with parents have the power to shape us. It gives me great peace to know that He is with them.

I have made many living amends in my life. To the best of my imperfect human ability, by loving others freely without condition, by being kind to all that I meet, by accepting others exactly as they are, and by doing the right thing no matter what, I was able to be a better example to my children than I was during my drinking.

I now see in them that same love, kindness, and acceptance of others. Humbly, that credit goes to their mother and to God, and to how God has chosen to use me in their lives.

I have loved my ex-wife with all my might, mind, and strength—always willing to be there if she needed me, always willing to lend a loving ear, always keeping a place in my heart that will always be reserved for her.

The people that I have hurt in my life may not have forgiven me perfectly or completely. How could they? Human forgiveness takes time. There are those in my life that I'm sure never forgave me. They may not even know they carry that burden. That is out of my hands now.

I have made all the direct amends that I possibly could. I have made all the indirect amends that I possibly could. I will continue living amends as long as I live, as I choose to do the next indicated right thing to the best of my ability and to the best of my human understanding.

3. Forgiveness

Because of His great sacrifice in the Atonement of Christ, we have been forgiven and can come home to Him and live with Him in eternity. He loves us so very much.

Now love yourself. You deserve your love. You deserve your forgiveness.

Jesus teaches forgiveness this way;

Matthew 18:21–35

"Then came Peter to Him, and said, Lord, how oft shall my brother sin against me, and I forgive him? till seven times? Jesus saith unto him,

I say not unto thee, Until seven times: but, Until seventy times seven.

Therefore is the kingdom of heaven likened unto a certain king, which would take account of his servants. And when He had begun to reckon, one was brought unto Him, which owed Him ten thousand talents. But for as much as he had not to pay, his Lord commanded him to be sold, and his wife, and children, and all that he had, and payment to be made. The servant therefore fell down, and worshiped Him, saying, Lord, have patience with me, and I will pay Thee all. Then the Lord of that servant was moved with compassion, and loosed him, and forgave him the debt.

But the same servant went out, and found one of his fellow servants, which owed him an hundred pence: and he laid hands on him, and took him by the throat, saying, Pay me that thou owest. And his fellow servant fell down at his feet, and besought him, saying, Have patience with me, and I will pay thee all. And he would not: but went and cast him into prison, till he should pay the debt. So when his fellow servants saw what was done, they were very sorry, and came and told unto their Lord all that was done.

Then his Lord, after that he had called him, said unto him, O thou wicked servant, I forgave thee all that debt, because thou desired me: Shouldest not thou also have had compassion on thy fellow servant, even as I had pity on thee? And his Lord was wroth, and delivered him to the tormentors, till he should pay all that was due unto him.

So likewise shall my heavenly Father do also unto you, if ye from your hearts forgive not every one his brother their trespasses."

After reading my personal inventory to another human being I still had to come to a point where I was willing to forgive those that had hurt me and become willing to forgive myself. I didn't need to forgive everyone and everything. I just needed to become willing to consider it. As we've learned, once we are willing, God can begin to work in us and through us in accordance with His will, plan, and timing.

Are you now willing to consider forgiving everyone, everything, and forgive yourself?

Forgiving Others: Pray for them

We don't need to forgive others completely or totally for everything they've done. We just need to be willing to do so. It doesn't need to happen instantaneously or overnight. We've carried this pain and resentment for a good long time. We've been betrayed, and hurt, and abandoned; these wounds are real and substantial and have shaped who we are and how we live. They have not only shaped us, but they have influenced those around us as well. We need to be willing, and we need God's help.

The process that I was taught, the one I will now share with you, works on so many different levels. It systematically changes the way I think and feel toward the person whose offense I am forgiving though repetition, but more importantly it brings God into it so He can heal our broken hearts.

What I want you to do is pray for the person that you need to forgive. I used this process to forgive all the people in my life that had hurt me. I also used this technique to overcome my negative feelings and thoughts toward the church, to government, and for humanity and all the atrocities committed to us by us. I was able to cleanse my soul from the stain of resentment.

"God, I come to Thee humbled and grateful for all the moments of my life.

I ask You Lord that You give me the willingness and courage to forgive this person.

I ask You Lord that You might bless this person, that You might love them, that You might comfort them.

I wish that You take everything I could ever hope for myself: a long, healthy, and happy life, peace, joy, a feeling of union and togetherness with those around me, success, direction, guidance, and more than everything Lord, hope, faith, and love, and an eternity spent with You.

Lord, I ask that You take all these things that I want for myself and I ask that, if it is Your will, that You give them all to them.

Lord, love them. Please, love them. Amen."

Say this prayer every day. Say it even if you don't mean it. Say it even if you don't want to. Say it in spite of your anger, say it in spite of your hatred, say it in spite of your condemnation. Just say it. Trust in the process. You're praying to God and bringing His perfect understanding and wisdom into this.

Say it every day and you'll see that as time progresses your attitude toward this person will begin to change. You'll see that your heart and your mind are beginning to heal. You'll begin to feel like you might actually mean it and want these things for this person. You'll begin to feel really good about wanting these things for another human being, for another Child of God, for your eternal brother or sister.

You'll begin to develop compassion toward this person. You'll begin to see that they, like you, are imperfect human beings, who suffer like you do, who hurts like you do, who has been, as you have been, lost and deceived for much of their lives. You'll begin to understand that if you had lived the life that they lived, endured the things they did, you might have acted in a similar fashion. You'll begin to see that they don't need our judgment, they need our love, and they need our forgiveness.

Saying this prayer daily for this person will strengthen your humility, driving pride out of your heart. It will strengthen your ability to love, driving fear out of your heart. It will strengthen your ability to hope, casting out impatience from your heart. It will strengthen your faith, casting doubt from your heart.

By praying for others, especially those who have harmed us, we bless them, but we also allow ourselves to be blessed. By praying for others, we do unto others and Jesus Christ would do, and as such we carry the torch of His ministry, which is wholly and completely a ministry of love.

Jesus teaches us;

Matthew 5:38–46 (KJV)

"Ye have heard that it hath been said, An eye for an eye, and a tooth for a tooth:
But I say unto you, That ye resist not evil: but whosoever shall smite thee on thy right cheek, turn to him the other also.
And if any man will sue thee at the law, and take away thy coat, let him have thy cloke also.
And whosoever shall compel thee to go a mile, go with him twain.
Give to him that asketh thee, and from him that would borrow of thee turn not thou away.

Ye have heard that it hath been said, thou shalt love thy neighbour, and hate thine enemy.
But I say unto you, Love your enemies, bless them that curse you, do good to them that hate you, and pray for them which despitefully use you, and persecute you;
That ye may be the children of your Father which is in heaven: for He maketh his sun to rise on the evil and on the good, and sendeth rain on the just and on the unjust."

You are His child, He loves you, He has already forgiven you. Now accept His grace and forgive yourself.

And I pray:

"God, my loving Heavenly Father, I offer myself to Thee with all that I am, with all that I ever will be.

Lord, I am an imperfect and flawed being. I have sinned against You and hurt others.

This cross of guilt and shame I carry with me weighs me down and pains me so.

Lord, if it be Thy will, allow me to set this cross down, that I might cease this struggle, that I might lay down my burdens, that I might finally forgive myself for my sins against myself.

Lord, love me. Please guide me toward Your truth. Please comfort me, oh Lord.

I ask these things with reverence through complete surrender, in the name of Your Son, Jesus Christ,

Amen."

Chapter 12 - His Grace is Sufficient

Grace Beyond Words

I found that as I tried to understand the exact nature of grace and the role of the Atonement of Christ in it, I was brought to the limits of human language—the complete inability of something imperfect to fully grasp and explain something eternal in nature. Like someone born blind trying to describe color, or someone born deaf trying to describe the greatest symphonies, we are simply unequipped to do so with any real accuracy or authority. Where language screams, "I've finally got it!" paradox sweeps in to silence it.

1 Corinthians 2:9–11 (KJV)

"But as it is written, Eye hath not seen, nor ear heard, neither have entered into the heart of man, the things which God hath prepared for them that love Him.
But God hath revealed them unto us by His Spirit: for the Spirit searcheth all things, yea, the deep things of God.
For what man knoweth the things of a man, save the spirit of man which is in him? even so the things of God knoweth no man, but the Spirit of God."

We attempt to use words to describe something that cannot be known without transformation—and even then, cannot be fully re-articulated in mortal language.

What we can do, with our limited human understanding and language, is describe how grace is experienced here in this mortal existence. There are words enough for that. The whole Bible is a collection of testimonies—witnesses describing what mental, emotional, and spiritual postures allow us to experience the love of God, and which postures keep us from it.

This book is not about understanding what grace is. It is about coming to a place where we can remember a state that existed before fear, before self-reliance, and before separation. It is about experiencing the fruits of that state in this mortal life and being restored to it fully in eternity.

Where the limits of human language, understanding, and effort end, that is where the gift of the Atonement of Christ steps in. Where our best efforts fail us is where Christ's sacrifice saves us. We do not need to know metaphysically what was done or how it was done. We do not need all the answers. In fact, not having all the answers is part of the point. We do not need to understand the nature of something in order to experience it. We do not need to know why the light turns on when we flip the switch—only that when we do, the light will surely come.

Isaiah 55:8–9 (KJV)

"For my thoughts are not your thoughts, neither are your ways my ways, saith the LORD.
For as the heavens are higher than the earth, so are my ways higher than your ways, and my thoughts than your thoughts."

Grace is not something God began giving after the Fall as a reward for righteousness; it is part of a relationship with a loving Father that, through pride, we forgot was always there—a relationship that the Atonement of Christ restores to our remembrance. Grace is not merely God's gift, but God's gift that restores us to communion with Him—a communion we once shared, lost through pride, and can now re-enter through the Atonement of Christ.

John 17:21–23 (KJV)

"That they all may be one; as Thou, Father, art in me, and I in Thee, that they also may be one in us: that the world may believe that Thou hast sent me.
And the glory which Thou gavest me I have given them; that they may be one, even as we are one:
I in them, and Thou in me, that they may be made perfect in one; and that the world may know that Thou hast sent me, and hast loved them, as Thou hast loved me."

So how do we experience this communion with God here in our mortal existence? This whole book has led you to this moment. Remember what you have read and learned and experienced up to this point.

Through willingness, acceptance, surrender, faith, hope, and love—and by laying down the burdens that prevent us from being willing, accepting, surrendering, having faith, having hope, and loving as He did — we can enter into a life of growing alignment and harmony with Him.

2 Corinthians 12:7–10 (KJV)

"And lest I should be exalted above measure through the abundance of the revelations, there was given to me a thorn in the flesh, the messenger of Satan to buffet me, lest I should be exalted above measure.
For this thing I besought the Lord thrice, that it might depart from me.
And He said unto me, My grace is sufficient for thee: for my strength is made perfect in weakness. Most gladly therefore will I rather glory in my infirmities, that the power of Christ may rest upon me.
Therefore I take pleasure in infirmities, in reproaches, in necessities, in persecutions, in distresses for Christ's sake: for when I am weak, then am I strong."

And that is sufficient for me.

"Enough, Kyle. It's enough. All of the moments of your life have been forgiven"

Conclusion

This book was never meant to remove every burden you will ever carry. Life will continue to present moments of fear, grief, anger, desire, doubt, and pain. That is not failure. That is being human.

You may still be holding onto many things, and that's okay. You may carry burdens you don't yet know how to release. If you offer them to Him, He will help you. There may be something within you that feels too heavy to overcome; trust in the One who has all power and loves you beyond words. This, too, shall pass.

Laying burdens down is not a single moment of surrender but a lifelong decision to choose love over pride. Again and again, we will forget, pick up, carry, and hold onto something we do not need to carry or hold onto; God steps in, and we remember that we no longer need it, that we are indeed forgiven, and that we are now free to rest in Him.

There is no need for impatience, as God's timing is perfect. The process of preparation will take you the rest of your life.

You are not behind or lacking, you are exactly where and what you are supposed to be exactly at this moment.

The invitation remains the same today as it has always been and always will be:

Come unto Him.
Lay the burden down.
And enjoy the joy that is your birthright.

And I pray:

"Your Grace is sufficient for me, Your strength is made perfect in my weakness.

I pray Lord that I might be weak. I don't want to be strong any longer. I don't want to be right. I don't want to be recognized. I don't want to be exalted.

I don't need to understand. I don't need to know the truth. I don't need to be perfect.

I don't need joy. I don't need happiness. I don't need comfort. I don't need companionship. I don't need credit. I don't need fame. I don't need to be morally superior. I don't need to teach anyone anything.

I just need You. I just need You Lord.

It's all I want. That's it.

Your will. Your plan. Your timing.

Give me faith Lord, give me hope Lord, but above all else Lord, give me love, that I might give back that which You have so graciously given, This great gift and blessing that is Your Presence.

Thank You Lord, thank You, thank You, thank You.

I humbly and meekly ask these things in the name of Your Son, my Savior and Redeemer, Jesus Christ,

Amen."

THE END

www.ingramcontent.com/pod-product-compliance
Lightning Source LLC
LaVergne TN
LVHW051000080826
845145LV00009B/2382

* 9 7 8 1 7 3 7 4 7 3 2 3 7 *